PRAISE

It's a Wonderful
(Imperfect) Life

Joan's message is one of freedom for a culture burdened by feelings of guilt and imperfection. Each page speaks straight to the heart of learning to live in the unfailing grace of God. Oh, what a relief it is!

Marsha Crockett
Author of *Break Through: Unearthing God's Image to Find the Real You*

It's a Wonderful (Imperfect) Life provides a daily dose of reality by reminding us that God is God . . . and we are not. With true wisdom, candor and just the right touch of humor, Joan's devotions are brief enough to fit any schedule but deep enough to help readers stop, think and breathe a sigh of relief: There is room in God's world to be human; there is room in God's world to be *me*.

Vicki Kuyper
Speaker and author of *Wonderlust* and *Breaking the Surface*
www.vickikuyper.com

I'm relieved, inspired and uplifted. This is a message to encourage every Christian who struggles. It's just perfect!

Debbie Macomber
New York Times bestselling author
www.debbiemacomber.com

Here's your daily dose of stress-reducing, pressure-releasing, life-changing hope. Author Joan Webb helps you "baby step" away from the pitfalls of perfectionism so you can stop obsessing over details and start enjoying every day. Put this powerful little book at the top of your reading—and gift-giving—list!

Debi Stack
Humorous speaker and author of *Martha to the Max: Balanced Living for Perfectionists* and *Smotherly Love.*™

It's a Wonderful (Imperfect) Life

Life

Devotional Readings for Women
Who Strive Too Hard to Make It Just Right

JOAN C. WEBB

Regal

From Gospel Light
Ventura, California, U.S.A.

Published by Regal
From Gospel Light
Ventura, California, U.S.A.
www.regalbooks.com
Printed in the U.S.A.

Published in association with the literary agency of WordServe Literary Group, Ltd., 10152 S. Knoll Circle, Highlands Ranch, CO 80130.

Library of Congress Cataloging-in-Publication Data
Webb, Joan C., 1948-
It's a wonderful (imperfect) life : devotional readings for women who strive too hard to make it just right / Joan C. Webb.
p. cm.
ISBN 978-0-8307-4801-3 (trade paper)
1. Christian women—Prayers and devotions. 2. Perfectionism (Personality trait)—Religious aspects—Christianity—Meditations. I. Title.
BV4844.W43 2009
242'.643—dc22
2008051864

Rights for publishing this book outside the U.S.A. or in non-English languages are administered by Gospel Light Worldwide, an international not-for-profit ministry. For additional information, please visit www.glww.org, email info@glww.org, or write to Gospel Light Worldwide, 1957 Eastman Avenue, Ventura, CA 93003, U.S.A.

*I lovingly dedicate this book to
my dad, Bob Pressler, who introduced me to
Jesus, the Author of Grace, when I was seven
years old—and who has been my prayer
support ever since*

and

*Calissa Jolie Rasmussen, my youngest
granddaughter, who decided to come into the world
while I wrote these pages. May you be touched by
the grace and compassion of Christ through
each stage of your life.*

Contents

Preparing for Relief:
Freedom, Here I Come!

The Relief of Imperfect Relationships and Families:
It's Not My Job!

The Relief of Imperfect
Emotions, Minds and Bodies:
Exquisitely Intertwined

The Relief of Imperfect Life-Work and Service:
Regaining Life

The Relief of Imperfect Churches and Culture:
No Formula Solutions

The Relief of Imperfect
Dreams, Plans and Decisions:
The Joy of the Imperfect Yes!

The Relief of Imperfect
Faith, Prayer and Spirituality:
Striving Too Hard Dulls Your Soul

The Promise of Relief:
Breathing Room for Your Soul

Appreciation

Huge thanks to Kim Bangs and the incredibly creative team at Regal Books. I appreciate your flexibility during this writing adventure. Thank you to my literary agent, Greg Johnson, and his wife and partner, Becky Johnson. Your hard work and encouragement mean so much to me.

How grateful I am for my colleagues and friends in the Intentional Woman Network (www.intentionalwoman.org): Cathy Roberts, Catherine Antone, Kristina Bailey, Lisa Gifford, Gayle Gilbertson, Kelli Gotthardt, Grayce Gusmano, Holly Hart, Tina Henningson, Teresa Perrine, Annie Thompson, Audrey Thorkelson and Carol Travilla. Your prayers and email support spurred me on.

I'm always inspired by the stories, anecdotes and insights that my coaching and life-plan partners share with me. Your wisdom influenced these devotions. Thank you. I wrote *It's a Wonderful (Imperfect) Life* in a relatively short time-span, so I chose to put my cherished studies and get-togethers on temporary "hold." Thanks to Mary Pierce, Marsha Crockett and Sue Theobald for your patience, understanding and prayers. Gratitude to Madeline, Ernie and Brenda at Strawberry Retreat Center for my "writing-home-away-from-home." Thank you again to Herb and Beth Rawling for sharing your time-share condo so that I could get away to write.

Thank you to Kristina Bailey, my life coach, friend and fellow Intentional Woman presenter, for splashing my life with grace, relief and loads of listening. I appreciate the competent help of my assistant, Sarah LaScala. Thank you immensely to those who signed up to be on my email prayer team: Beth Fleming, Cheryl King, Marsha Crockett, Len and Pauly Rodgers, Arlene Johnston—and to the countless others who joined in praying.

And to my family—please know that I missed being with you when I was away on those writing retreats. Just hearing your voices on the telephone relaxed and encouraged me. Love and gratitude to you all. Daughter Lynnette Rasmussen—your perseverance during your challenging pregnancy and delivery encouraged me to practice patience with my process, too. Thank you to son-in-law Adam Rasmussen and son Rich Webb and his understanding wife, Anne Webb. I appreciate your support, prayers and love.

From across the miles, I felt the prayerful support of my father, Bob Pressler, and sisters, Patty Brock and Karen Boothe, and their families. And special "grandma gratitude" to my loving and enthusiastic grandchildren: Annika, Max, Kirsten, Luke, Lesia, Sam and Calissa. You bring such joy into my life. And to my husband, Richard—words are inadequate to express how much I appreciate, love and respect you. Your gracious support and prayers made this whirlwind writing project possible. I love you.

A Note from Joan

Dear Reader-Friend,

I'd love to sit and chat with you face to face for a few moments. However, since that isn't possible, I'm writing you this note instead. And as I write, I'm enjoying listening to Christmas carols in the background.

It's that time of year again—when we celebrate Christ's birthday. I'm surrounded by twinkling lights on the Christmas tree, garlands lining the windows, and fragrant (cinnamon-vanilla!) candles. It's wonderful, but everything's not perfect. I haven't had time to color-coordinate the gift wrapping (something I really enjoy doing) or make cookies (that's not my favorite thing to do, anyway!). Because I had no star or angel for the top of the tree this year, I created a makeshift topper. The Webb family Christmas celebration, with our two children, son-in-law and daughter-in-law, and seven grandchildren, is tomorrow night (December 17), so that means Richard and I will spend a very quiet Christmas Day. We chose to do it this way so that our children can spend Christmas week with their in-laws. This is evidence that a woman who had a tendency to *strive too hard to make it all just right* really can change! Because I'm fine—well, more than fine—with all this slightly imperfect holiday reality.

Hey, there's no perfect way to celebrate Christmas. And there's no perfect way to enjoy this devotional book, either. You don't have to read it in chronological order, yet you can if you like. Maybe you'll read it from back to front, or skip around. It doesn't matter.

The devotions are grouped into categories, including relationships, emotions, bodies, life-work, service, churches, culture, dreams and spirituality. If you're wishing for a little grace and relief in any of these life areas, jump right into that section. At the end of each devotion, I have added a "Make It Personal" question or follow-up activity. As I assure my coaching clients, you have options for responding: You can say *yes* or *no* to the suggestions, or you can renegotiate your response or think about it and come back to it later—or not at all. You may jot your thoughts in the page margins of this book or in a separate journal.

There are no specific "shoulds" or "have tos." Just enjoy *It's a Wonderful (Imperfect) Life*.

And if you'd like to learn more about experiencing relief in the midst of your imperfect circumstances, you may wish to read one of my other books, *The Relief of Imperfection*.

Remember—life doesn't have to be perfect to be wonderful. I'm smiling here.

Relief blessings,
Joan

It's a Wonderful
(Imperfect)
Life

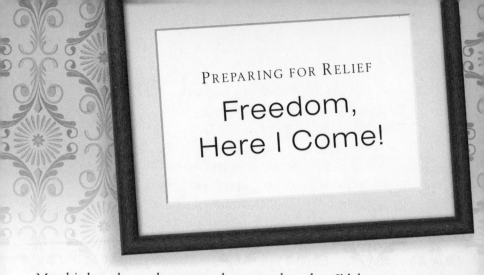

Freedom, Here I Come!

My third-grade teacher warned my mother that I'd have a nervous breakdown by the age of 18. Gratefully, she was wrong! However, I did burn out before reaching 40, oblivious that the *internal* and *external* unreasonable expectations I had about work, play, relationships, appearance and spirituality were depleting me. There's a freedom-robbing misconception floating around our homes, schools, businesses, churches and culture. It permeates our families, emotions, ministries, dreams and faith. This misconception? That people, things, organizations and circumstances have the capacity to be *just right* (that is, flawless). Notice the 24/7 bigger-better-more-faster ad saturation. Does the promotional tag-line "relentless pursuit of perfection" sound familiar?

The dictionary defines the word "perfection" as "the state of being complete in every way; without defect; flawless; completely accurate; pure, most excellent or faultless."[1] *So what's wrong with perfection?* Obviously, nothing. It defines the character of God. He is perfect in every possible way, each moment of every decade.

Sometimes I push my desire to be an excellent, committed Christian woman into my Creator's solo territory of perfection. I may long to live beyond my human limitations of time, space, skin and finite reasoning, but it just isn't possible. When I adopt—even in part—this misconception (that people, circumstances and things have the ability to be *just right*—or *perfect*), then life and others become a continual disappointment. Major bummer.

That same dictionary indicates that "perfectionism" (or striving too hard to make it all just right) is "the theory that moral, religious, or social perfection can be attained by mortals."[2] *Yikes!* Actually, perfectionism (I realize you might not relish being associated with that word—I don't, either!) is subtler than lining up canned goods in alphabetical order or insisting a report be edited endlessly. It's about unrealistic expectations—how we belittle ourselves and others for having human (we translate that as *weak*) thoughts and emotions, inconsistent faith, or *ordinary* accomplishments, families, bodies or choices.

The problem is that when we strive too hard to make it all just right, eventually we get bone-tired—and become candidates for physical, mental, emotional and spiritual burnout. Physicians who've noticed this growing trend have coined the phrase "hurried syndrome" to describe the various ailments they see in astounding frequency that are related to trying to do too much, too perfectly, in too little time.

Living in this bigger-better-more-faster culture, I've noticed something: This saturated, accomplishment-oriented philosophy often leads to an exaggerated sense of power and entitlement that can edge out God, faith, simple reality and joy.

The reality is that *people* (including friends, parents, children, spouses and ourselves), *circumstances* (including projects, work, vacations and quiet times) and *things* (including homes, body parts and ideas) do not have the ability to be flawless. *Perfection on this earth is not possible.* This may seem discouraging. Yet when this truth infiltrated my mind and gradually seeped into my soul, my shoulders relaxed and I gained permission to breathe more deeply.

It's truly a relief once you and I realize that God doesn't expect us to be, do or make it all just right, all the time, in order to be valuable and compassionate friends, mothers, colleagues or Christians. Perhaps you wonder about Jesus' words, "Be perfect" (Matthew 5:48). I did, too. It helped when I discovered that the original word for "perfect" means *to be committed to growth and completion.* While growth is daunting at times, it *is* doable. We can't change another, yet we can manage ourselves. It's okay with God if we slow down, relax and smile in the midst of our imperfect realities. *Life doesn't have to be perfect to be wonderful.*

I invite you to join me on this adventure to freedom from striving too hard to make it all just right. So here we go—I mean, here we *grow!*

Smiling Here

I saw myself so stupid. . . . But even so, you love me!
Psalm 73:22-23, *TLB*

Carefully, I made out the grocery list so that I wouldn't forget anything. Walking the aisles, I checked off each item as I put it in the grocery basket. When I came to the soft drink area, I consulted my list for the brand my family wanted. I reached for the appropriate 24-pack and loaded it in the cart. After reviewing the list, I smiled with a sense of completion. Then I checked out and drove home to put it all away.

As we were emptying the bags, I heard a groan.

"What's wrong?" I asked.

"You got caffeine-free *regular* soda instead of caffeine-free *diet* soda. How could you do that? Couldn't you tell the difference?"

Immediately I felt the shame. *I tried hard to please everyone by getting all the correct items. How could I have failed?*

Then, to my amazement, I heard these words come from my mouth: "Well, I guess I made a mistake."

My immediate personal thoughts? *I goofed. No big deal! It doesn't make me less valuable.* Surprised by my verbal response and new self-chatter, I realized the liberating truth: I was finally escaping the tyranny of my striving-too-hard-to-make-it-all-just-right mindset, and was learning to live with my humanness and imperfection. I couldn't help smiling. Still can't. And it's definitely a relief!

Lord, I release myself and others from the rigid rules of perfectionism, even in the little daily areas of our lives.

Make It Personal: Tell a good friend about a recent blunder you made. Chuckle about it together.

Easy Does It

That everyone may . . . find satisfaction in
all his toil—this is the gift of God.

Ecclesiastes 3:13

"Honey, you've had a busy day. Come watch the game with me," suggested my husband.

"In a minute."

Silently I added, *First, I gotta clean the kitchen, wash a load of clothes and finish tomorrow's report.* My promised "minute" evolved into several hours.

Speaker Robert J. Kriegel contends that "gottas" have become the chief reaction for many of us in our bigger-better-faster-more culture. "The Gotta's can run your life," writes Kriegel in his book *If It Ain't Broke . . . Break It!*[4]

I gotta *clean the house before company comes. I* gotta *study my Bible lesson. I* gotta *get an A on that test. I* must *start the kids on piano lessons. I* should *host the neighborhood party.* It can become a never-ending cycle of inner demands.

Obviously, you and I need to accomplish certain tasks in order to lead healthy lives (brushing our teeth, showering and eating, to name a few). However, when we let the *shoulds* and *gottas* control our lives, we lose our sense of contentment. God isn't the one who pressures us. He wants us to delight in our life and work—whatever it is at this season. Satisfaction and enjoyment are God's gifts to us.

Lord, I don't want to be confined by my "gottas,"
but getting rid of the excessive shoulds in my
vocabulary isn't easy. Please help me.

Make It Personal: Name three gottas that could keep you from enjoying this coming week. Now eliminate one of those gottas—just for the next few days. Easy does it.

To Be or Not to Be?

"What are the things God wants us to do?"
Jesus answered, "The work God wants you to do is this:
to believe in the One that God sent."
John 6:29, NCV

Lord, what do You want me to do? is a valid question, but sometimes we emphasize this query more than the essential one: *Lord, who do You want me to be?* When concentrating primarily on *doing* without allowing time to consider who I'm *becoming*, I can get overtired and agitated. It's a vicious cycle: I *do*, but it doesn't always produce the peace I crave, so I conclude that I should *do* more.

According to the Excellence vs. Perfectionism chart in *The Relief of Imperfection*, when you and I chase for perfection (striving too hard to make it all just right) our lives are shaped by the pursuit of *doing*.⁵ Yet when we partner with God for excellence—which is enjoying quality in balance—our lives focus on the pursuit of *being*.

This reminds me of when Jesus' followers asked, "What does God want us to *do*?" Jesus replied, "The work God wants you to do is *believe*." Jesus offers you and me relief from the performance merry-go-round. He assures us that God wants us to *be*—to be a believing person. We *believe* that He sent Jesus to show us His love. Being doesn't mean we neglect action. Doing flows naturally out of being. We can learn to *be* first and then *do*.

Lord, today I'll hit the pause button on my over-doing so that I can get quiet enough inside to acknowledge the growing faith within me.

Make It Personal: Who are you becoming?

Is It Burnout?

*He gives strength to the weary . . . those who hope
in the Lord will renew their strength.*

Isaiah 40:29,31

Caring, conscientious, goal-oriented and over-achieving women (and men, too!) are candidates for burnout. In case you think only executives who work too late and too hard can experience burnout, read the following definition. Burnout is "the type of stress and emotional fatigue, frustration, and exhaustion that occurs when a series of (or combination of) events in a relationship, mission, way of life, or job fail to produce an expected result."[6] Perhaps you recognize yourself or someone you know.

I felt positive that my commitment to hard work would bring me what I desired and was flabbergasted when I ran out of energy, enthusiasm and faith. Disillusioned, I asked: *Is there any hope for renewal?*

"Yes, Joan!" assured my loving Creator. "Though you stumble, you'll one day soar on wings like an eagle, run and not grow weary, walk and not faint. Trust Me. I'll renew your lost strength."[7] I didn't feel it or foresee it. I didn't even have the strength to believe it, but since I couldn't *do* it anymore, I stopped trying and left my *stuff* with God. Miraculously, when I stopped striving, God took over.

*Lord, at times I'm just too exhausted to feel.
I want to avoid further damage.
I'm asking for Your help.*

Make It Personal: Read the definition of burnout again. What part of it taps you on your shoulder (or maybe punched you in the stomach)? Write a brief example. Awareness is a positive step forward.

The Over-whatevered Life

*Call to me and I will answer you and tell you
great and unsearchable things.*

Jeremiah 33:3

If you dream of slowing down and mellowing but don't know how, you've probably been overtired for too long. No matter what your life season—recent graduate, newly retired, parent of toddlers, empty-nester, executive, ministry volunteer—you could be tumbling toward burnout.[8]

Jane Chesnutt, Editor-in-Chief at *Woman's Day* magazine, calls this predicament the "over-scheduled, over-worried, over-whatevered life."[9] Since awareness is a key step toward making positive changes, here are a few questions to help you gauge your current situation:

- Do you have a difficult time relaxing?
- Are you crankier than you used to be?
- Do you rush from one project to another?
- Are you exhausted on a regular basis?
- Are you increasingly angry and don't know why?
- Do you spend less time with friends and family?
- Do you work hard and long, but accomplish less?
- Is life becoming a drag, more times than not?

If you answered yes to several of these, burnout might be looming before you. It doesn't mean that you've always been here or that you'll stay forever. Still, the thought of adjusting your existing routine may seem frightening and overwhelming. Good news: There is a way. Acknowledge your need, ask for help and take active steps to reshape your thoughts and behavior. God waits patiently for your call.

Lord, I'm tired. Please give me courage to make the necessary changes.

Make It Personal: What helpful resources are available to you? Make a plan to contact one this week.

Today's Disappointment/ Tomorrow's Opportunity

And for your sake, I am glad I wasn't there, because this will give you another opportunity to believe in me. Come, let's go see him.

John 11:15, *NLT*

Recently, I discovered a new appetizer: edamame. I know that they are merely soybeans in a pod, but I crave them—anytime, anywhere. Yesterday, I bought a bag of frozen edamame and poured half the package into a bowl, setting them in the refrigerator to thaw. I planned to enjoy them as a bedtime snack. Later, I put the bowl in the microwave, pushed the button and promptly forgot, drifting off to sleep.

I opened the microwave this morning to heat my tea and saw my snack. I frowned. *What a waste.* Then I thought, *Try them anyway, Joan. Maybe they'll be okay.* So I popped each pod into my mouth and contently squeezed out every bean. Call me crazy, but I enjoyed the edamame for breakfast with my chai tea! My mistake turned into a pleasant morning surprise.

You might chuckle at this light-hearted story, yet it hints of a deeper truth: Sometimes our *but-it-didn't-turn-out-the-way-I-planned* experiences become tomorrow's possibilities. Jesus wasn't there when His friend Lazarus fell ill and died. Sisters Mary and Martha understandably grieved. Yet Jesus said, "There's an opportunity here. Believe Me" (see John 11:1-44).

Lord, I tend to panic when circumstances and people don't turn out the way I think they should. Please help me trust You for the opportunity beyond my disappointment.

Make It Personal: Recall a past disappointing experience that resulted in a worthwhile opportunity for you. What did you learn? How can this experience help you with a disappointing situation you're facing now?

Break Time

Then the word of the Lord came to Elijah:
"Leave here, turn eastward and hide in the Kerith Ravine . . .
I have ordered the ravens to feed you there."

1 Kings 17:2-4

"I'm just delivering a message, King Ahab," said Elijah, a capable, conscientious spokesman for God. "A drought's coming. No dew or rain for several more years." Most likely, sensitive Elijah found it stressful to deliver this negative news. God acknowledged this probability and provided a place where Elijah would be comforted and renewed. God didn't chide Elijah for his *unproductive* time in the valley.

To me, this story indicates that God won't be angry with me if I take a time-out. (Not the kind I give my grandkids as discipline, but the "retreat and rest" type.) I don't need to accomplish (or pray, or serve) endlessly with no recuperation time. When I have little energy left to give, God doesn't reject me. This freeing reality relaxes my shoulders. Yet still I find myself asking, *Do you really get it, Joan?*

Do *you* get it, friend? Perhaps you could say no to a weeknight meeting and go home to sit by the fireplace, to read a novel, to play a game, to enjoy a date with your spouse, to have coffee with a friend or to take a nap.

Maybe you've been working too hard. Like Elijah, you need a break. God is in control, and I promise, you won't mess up His universal plans if you step back and unwind. Go ahead. It's okay.

Lord, thanks for providing for me,
whether I'm busy or resting.

Make It Personal: What intentional activity or non-activity might recharge your batteries? When will you do that?

Harnessing the Power

*Some trust in chariots and some in horses,
but we trust in . . . God.*

Psalm 20:7

"What's up since you left the showroom? How you doing?" my client asked, referring to my recent resignation as president of a growing young company.

"I'm adjusting my life to include some balance," I replied. "Trying to learn to say no to working harder and longer. It's tough, though."

"Yeah, it *is* hard to say no sometimes, isn't it?" he responded. "I got picked up by the police on a drunk-driving charge recently." He stared out the window. "I guess we all have to find a way to cope. Drinking's mine; maybe working is yours."

We need something bigger than ourselves to help us deal with life's harsh realities. The psalmist wrote about those who trusted in chariots and horses. Over-working, over-drinking, over-helping and just plain striving too hard to make it all just right can give us a similar sense of power. We may harness and ride this power to handle our fear, frustration and disappointment that life hasn't turned out the way we believed it should.

Yet perhaps like I have, you've discovered that these power sources turned on us, that they betray us. God is our reliable—and compassionate—power source. You and I can find strength in accepting our weakness and releasing ourselves to God.

*Lord, the power sources I trusted have failed me.
You are stronger. Although I know I won't do it perfectly,
I want to trust You instead.*

Make It Personal: When do you find it difficult to say no? This week say no at least 10 times.

Finding the Fun

I saw something . . . that was senseless. I saw a person . . .
He always worked hard. But he was never satisfied with what
he had. He never asked himself, "For whom am I working
so hard? Why don't I let myself enjoy life?"

Ecclesiastes 4:7-8, NCV

"I gotta go," said a college student whom I mentored. "If I don't get it all done, I'll be toast!"

"What's up?" I asked.

"I needed to read five chapters, finish a report, research job openings online, write a letter to my fiancé and call my grandmother. It's her birthday."

"How much is left to do?" I asked.

"Well, I'm done with all that. But I really need to be further along. I gave up last night's waitressing job, tips and all, so I could get ahead."

Some of us feel like we're always on the brink of disaster even though we experience obvious success. Rather than congratulate ourselves for reaching our goals, we change the rules. Rather than be satisfied with our progress, we demand better. *More! Harder! Faster!*

We're accustomed to cracking the whip, but tired of continually missing the celebration. Altering the way we think and work feels strange—and scary. Yet with patience and practice, we can learn to stop mistreating ourselves, value our accomplishments and enjoy life. It really *is* acceptable to God.

Lord, temper my striving to work harder, faster, longer
and MORE! I want to learn to take pleasure in my daily tasks
and achievements. Help me find the fun.

Make It Personal: Since you are going to live this day anyway, how can you make it fun?

Running on Empty

He has satisfied the thirsty soul,
and the hungry soul He has filled.

Psalm 107:9, *NASB*

I glanced at the gas gauge. *I'll make it,* I reasoned. *Can't stop now.* Not long later the red warning light blinked on. *Uh-oh, really low. Probably should stop and get gas. No time, though. I think I can make it to the next exit.*

But I didn't. The car sputtered and rolled to a stop. No gas, no power, no go. "Bummer. Wish I'd heeded the warning," I muttered as I started the hike to the gas station I had passed several miles ago.

"In the busyness of our day and life, it may seem like a waste of time to slow down, to stop what we're doing, and take [a] break. It is no more a waste of time than stopping to put gas in our car when the tank is almost empty," writes Melody Beattie in *The Language of Letting Go.*[10]

God doesn't expect me to run my life on empty. (You, either!) He promises to replenish our longing souls and refresh our minds and bodies. So let's decelerate when we notice the warning signs, turn off the speedway and fill up. We can get back on the road later.

Lord, my red warning light is flashing.
Help me slow down and fill up before
I run out of inner strength.

Make It Personal: What keeps you from stopping to fill up your inner tank? With this knowledge in mind, consider making a plan to turn off the speedway and refuel—even for 15 minutes. While you're resting and filling up your inner tank, take several deep breaths.

Lazy? Not!

*Never be lacking in zeal, but keep your
spiritual fervor, serving the Lord.*

Romans 12:11

"Not slothful in business, [but] fervent in spirit" (Romans 12:11, *KJV*).
I underlined that phrase in my Bible. Perish the possibility that anyone
would call me lazy or slothful! And cherish the thought everyone might
find me zealous, fervent and hard working. I've noticed that others like
me (perfectionists, that is, although I still dislike that word!) use Scrip-
tures like this one to support over-scheduling and over-doing. But does
this verse really encourage us to continue striving too hard to make it
all just right? I think not.

A truly slothful or lazy person makes inactivity and idleness a daily
habit. That's not me. And since you're reading this book, it's probably
not you, either! So here's the truth: We need not fear becoming lazy
when we add balance to our work and service. We make the best use
of our time and abilities by pausing to recoup as we develop our God-
given opportunities and invest our personal capital. The assets in your
personal capital account include your history, abilities, gifts, pain, for-
given sins, accomplishments, friendships, family, network, spiritual
growth and reputation. We have the privilege and opportunity to opti-
mize our personal capital.[11]

Through the availability of God's energizing Spirit, we can learn to
work and serve with enthusiasm and then rest at the appropriate times
without feeling guilty.

*Lord Jesus, while You were on earth, You were enthusiastic, zealous
and diligent, though not obsessively demanding or unbalanced.
Help me release my fear of appearing lazy and learn to live as You did.*

Make It Personal: Jot down at least five assets from your personal capital account.

Lighten Up

Relax, everything's going to be all right; rest, everything's
coming together; open your hearts, love is on the way!

Jude 1:2, *THE MESSAGE*

Me? A hippie? Absurd. I'm Ms. Responsibility—intense, direct, precise,
conscientious. Fun for me is research, strategy, accomplishment. So I
was surprised when my life-coaching instructor suggested that I take
on a "hippie" persona during a training exercise. To others, he assigned
characters like *princess, CEO* and *adolescent.* Joan became a *flower child.*

During a one-on-one role-play (with me as a hippie), I coached
Sam[12] and sensed resistance with his "I don't know" and "That won't
work" responses. Reporting later in the group, I said, "I honestly don't
care what he does. If he doesn't want to be coached, fine. It's his choice.
No big deal."

Silence. Then rumbling laughter. "Really good, Hippie Joan," ob-
served the instructor. Such a simple exercise, but the internal message
I received that day represented a turning point for me: *Lighten up, Joan.
It doesn't all depend on you. God doesn't expect you to make it all just right for
anyone else. Breathe, relax and enjoy.*

God grants abundant mercy (acceptance instead of condemna-
tion), peace (rest in place of zealous attempts to win God's favor) and
love (undiminished by how I perform).[13] As someone whose over-trying
can squeeze the life out of a project, desire or God-given assignment,
this knowledge is faith-filled relief.

Lord, it's fine to relax a little, isn't it?

Make It Personal: When you feel the urge to over-try, over-do, over-
expect or over-help, consider role-playing (with a friend or in your journal). Respond to one of your current dilemmas as if you were a
10-percent, 15-percent or even 25-percent hippie. Watch what happens.

Merely a Theory

There is no difference. For all have sinned,
and come short of the glory of God.

Romans 3:23, *KJV*

We've already discovered one definition of perfectionism (or striving too hard to make it just right) is "the theory that moral, religious, or social perfection can be attained by mortals." It's merely a theory, yet some of us have lived like we believe this notion—and it's worn us down.

Do you get impatient inside when a loved one's behavior doesn't meet your expectations? *I admit, I have.* Are you secretly certain that your ideas are best? *No comment.* Do you ever berate yourself for having unspiritual thoughts and feelings? *Well, yes, but I do it less now.* Have you ever wanted to hide when you made a mistake? *Duh!* Do you avoid situations and conversations that put you at risk for doing it "wrong"? *I still do sometimes, though I've made progress in this area, too.*

See why I call myself a "recovering perfectionist"?

Relief comes when I accept (not just nod at) this truth: *God is perfect. I'm not.* Paul writes in Romans 3:22-23 that no matter who you are or what you've done, it doesn't matter—everyone is unsuccessful at measuring up to God's perfect standards. We misinterpret His flawless ways and lack what it takes to possess the grandeur and faultless character of God. We *all* need God's redemptive love. In this truth, we're released to cease striving and accept God's mercy and rest.

God, I'm relieved I don't have to keep up this façade.
Only You are perfect. I need You.

Make It Personal: Stop and talk with God about what you're learning.

Clandestine Perfectionism

Then you will know the truth, and the truth will set you free.
John 8:32

"I don't consider myself a perfectionist, so I needn't worry about that," said a likeable young mother. "Just look at my messy house. On second thought—don't. I avoid inviting people over, because I've got unfinished projects scattered everywhere."

If I had a dollar for every time I've heard the "I'm not a perfectionist" claim, I'd be rich. (Not *really* rich, but I could buy a lot of groceries!)

As you'll notice from reading these devotions, striving too hard to make it all just right (perfectionism) can impact many areas of life: relationships, bodies, emotions, life-work, service, dreams, churches, faith. Yet some may not realize that procrastination lurks as a clandestine form of perfectionism. Covert perfectionists may not complete school, take that job, make a doctor's appointment or organize their kitchen. They may avoid creating new friendships, buying a house, singing in the choir, calling a counselor or teaching Sunday School, because they're afraid of making a mistake, being laughed at, appearing inadequate, failing—or even succeeding. Pushed to the extreme, making nearly any decision paralyzes procrastinators and procrastination becomes a lifestyle. Although it may seem like a laid-back approach to life, it's often painful and confining.

However, we *can* learn to believe a truth that will progressively free us from the procrastination trap: "I'm not perfect, yet Jesus loves me. His death has set me free, and I'm valuable in God's eyes."

Lord, I want to live free. Please help me.

Make It Personal: Consider doing the hard thing first each morning—or, as an option, right after lunch.

Making Reasonable Decisions

*What I'm trying to do here is get you to relax, not be so
preoccupied with getting so you can respond to God's giving. . . .
Don't be afraid of missing out. You're my dearest friends!*
Luke 12:29-32, *THE MESSAGE*

"I started with a genuine desire to help and make significant contributions before I left this world. Yet as years whizzed past and my goals remained unfulfilled, I felt compelled to hurry and *make* it happen," said my coworker.

She's not alone. Some of us want to make more money to give away, so we stay up later and work longer. Others of us increase our efforts to serve when people and organizations don't turn out the way we think they should. Trying harder seems to make sense. Regrettably, it doesn't produce the hoped-for results and we pay the price physically, emotionally and spiritually. What's up?

Carol Travilla, author of *Caring Without Wearing*, lists several unreasonable expectations that contribute to this dilemma: (1) There shouldn't be any limits to what I can do; (2) I'm the only person available to help; and (3) I have the ability to change another person.[14] We don't have to try to do the impossible. We can make reasonable choices, releasing this fear that we're missing out—or not doing enough. You and I are friends with God, and He invites us to relax in His generosity.

*Lord, I'm grateful to be called Your friend.
Please help me make relaxed and reasonable decisions about
my work, service and contributions.*

Make It Personal: When were your actions last week unreasonable? Name one way you can change that during the coming week.

Irrigating Your Soul

Blessed is the man who trusts in the Lord, whose
confidence is in him. He will be like a tree planted by the water
that sends out its roots by the stream.

Jeremiah 17:7-8

When our children were babies, we lived in the desert (Bakersfield, California). Dust and rolling sagebrush blew across the fields around our house. However, a built-in sprinkler system kept our yard lush and green. When the temperature topped 100 degrees day after day, we didn't worry about our flowers or fruit trees, as long as there was this consistent flow of water. (Then we moved to Minnesota and faced an entirely different weather situation!)

In recent years, we have moved back to the desert near Phoenix, Arizona. Although I don't have grass in my yard here, I plant seasonal flowers in large pots. I can always tell when our carefully placed water lines are clogged, because the blooms wilt and then turn crispy.

It reminds me of my recovery from burnout. I felt like I was trying to install a sprinkler system in a scorched wasteland. But Jeremiah's words gave me hope. God wants me to be blessed and joyous, not overworked and dried-up inside.

As I began to heave my burdens on Him, I noticed that my parched spirit slowly regained fresh life. I clung to the hope that I would once again be healthy, producing fruit—not merely by determined performance and over-doing, but by God's power within me.

Lord, I know I can't water my spirit alone.
I accept Your help.

Make It Personal: Every time you take a drink of water today, pray for God to irrigate your soul.

Don't Like the Upkeep

In the beginning God created.

Genesis 1:1

While driving down an old country road one day, a surprising thought popped into my mind: *JC, no wonder you're tired, edgy and perplexed; you've been attempting to do the impossible by molding your world and its inhabitants into perfection—trying to re-create according to your own vision and image. The job's too big for you.*

"Yikes, Lord," I whispered, "forgive me for trying to craft myself a perfect life—perfect family, perfect surroundings, perfect relationships, perfect work, perfect faith. I'm trespassing on Your territory and I don't like the upkeep, so I'm going to leave it to You!"

Although this insight seemed to appear out of nowhere, perhaps it originated from the Genesis study I was currently enjoying with my friends. I learned that the Hebrew word for "create" used in the first verse of the Bible is *bara*. This is a God-word. Human beings remain incapable of producing this way. Creating, out of nothing, is God's mission alone.

Trying to design myself a perfect world in which to live wore me out. What a relief to learn that it's not my responsibility.

Master Creator, I acknowledge that occasionally I interfere in
Your creation process. You're the all-knowing One, not me.
I want to be satisfied to be one of Your "created" and not the one
responsible for re-creation. So I'll leave the crafting process to You.

Make It Personal: What God-responsibility will you release back to Him this week? Write it down. Consider sharing your decision with a non-judgmental friend or mentor and ask her to check with you later to discuss how it turned out.

Hushing the Bully

You, Lord, give true peace . . . to those who trust you.

Isaiah 26:3, *NCV*

"If I fail to stay in high gear, I'm afraid everyone and everything will turn on me," said a colleague. "I just don't want to let anyone down."

Like this hard-working teacher, perhaps you sense a judge and jury peering over your shoulder. Maybe you have someone who pushes you beyond reasonable limits. Or perhaps the bully is in your own head. I identify with both scenarios. But here's the deal: In either case, I have a choice.

I can choose *not* to be bullied by myself or others. When I learn not to be controlled by unrealistic expectations and refuse to react with panic to sudden unplanned circumstances, my shoulders relax and I breathe better!

My best at any given moment in any specific situation is all I have. Although my best may vary according to the unique conditions of each situation, that's okay. My best is fine. *And so is yours.* We can admit the fear that our personal contributions to life won't be good enough. Then, with God's help, we can move past the panic to live in peace.

Lord, I'm committed to learning to chill out and trust You.
I really want to cooperate with You in silencing my inner bully
and reducing the negative power that the internal and external
slave drivers have in my life. Keep reminding me that my
okay-ness comes from You.

Make It Personal: What is your inner bully's name? Visualize telling him or her to sit down and hush. Now walk away and leave him or her sitting alone.

Pretending No More

For while we are in this tent [body], we groan and
are burdened . . . but God has given us the Spirit as a
deposit, guaranteeing what is to come.

2 Corinthians 5:4-5

"I thought that if I loved like I *should* and obeyed Jesus' teachings that I'd never allow disappointment, negativity or wrong to upset my life or my family," shared a friend. "I felt responsible for making sure we had no—or very few—problems. Regrettably, this meant I pretended a lot."

I identified with my friend. Larry Crabb, author of *Inside Out*, suggests that "we learn to pretend that we feel now what we cannot feel until Heaven. . . . The promise of one day being with Jesus in a perfect world is the Christian's only hope for complete relief. Until then we either groan or pretend we don't."[15]

You and I live in an imperfect world. We struggle daily with inadequate bodies, disappointing relationships and incomplete spirituality. Yet in the midst of this frustrating reality, we have a perfect God who gives us a comforting and strength-giving Helper. This is God's guarantee that, one day, all the groaning will be over.

Lord, I'm tired of pretending that everything
and everyone is perfect. Although my own limitations—
and others' inadequacies—irritate me sometimes, I'm going
to drop the façade. I'll enjoy Your Spirit's work in my life
while waiting for that future perfect day with You.

Make It Personal: Name a particular time when you sensed God's Spirit giving you comfort or insight. On a sticky note, jot a word that reminds you of that experience and put it where you'll see it this week.

My Walking Companion

Enoch walked with God 300 years.

Genesis 5:22

When my friend Sue flies from Minnesota to visit me in Arizona, we like to take walks together. Sometimes we take off in the morning (before it heats up around here), yet more often, we head out at dusk or after dark. We travel at the same pace, agree on what direction to go, experience the same scenery and enjoy one another's company.

Our walks remind me of a simple Bible phrase that changed my life years ago: *Enoch walked with God 300 years.* Enoch and God took a walk that lasted over three centuries! It couldn't have been a sprint, for a person cannot keep up that high-intensity pace for a sustained time period. There's no indication that Enoch and God walked together because Enoch had superior abilities, flawless determination, great intelligence, a perfect personality or a successful business. Instead, Enoch trusted his walking companion and God enjoyed His, too (see Hebrews 11:5).

After reading Enoch's short story in Genesis, I decided that I want to walk with God—not in a harried, I-must-impress-Him-with-my-devotion-and-speed attitude, but with relaxed confidence. At the end of my human life in this imperfect world, I want it to be said of me: *Joan walked with God.*

As you and I walk with God and our walk becomes a long-term adventure, we better understand His faultless character, love and acceptance. And our own relentless drive to make it all just right fades away. Now that's relief.

Lord, I want to walk with You.

Make It Personal: Make a simple plan to enjoy God's company during this coming week. Don't worry about the week after that yet.

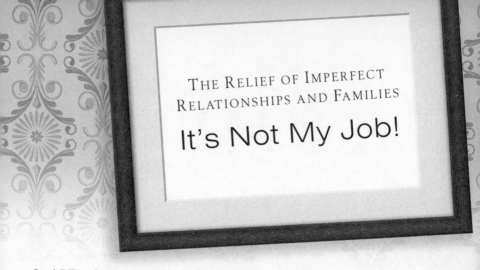

THE RELIEF OF IMPERFECT RELATIONSHIPS AND FAMILIES
It's Not My Job!

Joy! I Don't Have to Fix It All—Including You![16]

As I finished speaking, a young woman met me at the front of the crowd-packed room. Loudly, she said, "You're not going to like this, but . . ." She detailed everything she disagreed with. I thought we meshed on most issues, so I recapped the talking points I wanted her to grasp. Soon I realized I had increased her agitation instead of helping, so I simply stopped and said, "You didn't agree with a word I said, did you?"

The fire left her eyes and she smiled broadly. "No, I didn't. Sorry." Then she walked out the door.

That day, a relief-producing truth began to transform my relationships: *I don't have to be it all, fix it all, understand it all or make sure others understand it all. It's not my job.* As the pressure subsided, joy came rushing in. I'm not responsible for another's reactions, whether that person is a family member, friend, coworker or someone I've never met before. I can express my beliefs and when someone doesn't agree, I needn't try to change her—or silently judge her. *Oh, joy!* Yet my conditioned need to over-help caused me to wonder if I'd heard God correctly—which leads me to a second story.

One day, as Jesus was speaking, an affluent young man asked, "What should I do to guarantee I'll live forever?" After some interaction, Jesus saw the man's main need and said, "To mature spiritually and join God in heaven, sell what you have, share it and follow Me." This stunned the prosperous young man, so he turned his back on Jesus (and God!) and walked away.

What happens next astounds me: *Jesus watched him go.* He didn't run after the young man, tell another parable or try to alter his thinking. Jesus respected his decision and left the responsibility for growth where it belonged: with the young man (see Mark 10:17-30).

Both Jesus and I experienced results that neither of us would consider perfect.

We may yearn for 24/7, absolutely agreeable, support-filled and anxiety-free relationships in our ministries, families, work and friendships, but it isn't possible. Imperfect people living in a flawed world do not make perfect partnerships, marriages, families or churches. We may experience useful, loving, encouraging moments, but they won't be perfect all the time. To expect it is unrealistic. I recognize this, yet still I admit that it's often confusing how perfectionism, trying too hard and over-helping connect.

I find clarity by reviewing a chart, found in *The Relief of Imperfection*, that contrasts the difference between trying too hard to make it all just right (perfectionism) and partnering with God for excellence.[17] When we believe that we have power to fix another's problems, feelings or spirituality, we live in a fantasy. Motivated by fear of failure, avoiding anything negative and controlled by others' opinions, we play the comparison game. It wears us out. Once we adopt the lie that people have the ability to be perfect, our relationships become a constant disappointment. This way of life works *against* us.

Yet when we partner with God for excellence (that is, enjoying quality in balance) we dwell in reality and expect the best of ourselves as the women God designed us to be. It's doable and reasonable. We accept responsibility for our own growth and release our loved ones from the burden of making us happy and contented. Relief, air, relaxation and joy flood our relationships.

Even Jesus wasn't born into a perfect situation, community or family. With Him as our example, we can stop the silent demand that imperfection go away; we can unclench our hearts and enjoy one another. Relationships do not have to be perfect to be rewarding.

Uncomplicated Delight

God is more powerful than man is.
Ecclesiastes 6:10, *NCV*

I sat in the auditorium next to the guests I'd invited to join me for this special event. While engrossed in the beautiful music, it dawned on me: *Joan, you're enjoying this concert for the sheer pleasure of it, without being pre-occupied with your guests' thoughts, feelings or reactions.* I smiled then and I'm smiling now as I remember.

For years, an overzealous sense of responsibility overshadowed my personal enjoyment. When I invited another person to attend a church service, concert or even a luncheon, I felt duty-bound to see that she enjoyed the time and gained new insight. Now I realize that I'm not responsible for someone else's perceptions, attitudes or knowledge.

Through my years of life coaching and speaking, I've noticed an epidemic of over-helping. Those of us who want to join God in His work sometimes live by a false premise that we *must* fix what's broken, heal what hurts and right what's wrong (in our opinion). This over-active sense of responsibility can lead us to believe that we're more powerful than we really are. It's exhausting.

God is the Almighty One, and He wants to release us from this unnecessary responsibility. He is the one in charge of the world, not us. When we give Him our *shoulds, musts* and *ought-tos*, we begin to live in genuine freedom. What uncomplicated delight!

Lord, I'm not responsible for anyone else's life fulfillment.
Only my own.

Make It Personal: Jot down an unreasonable *I should* or *I must* that has worn you out and threatened to keep you from experiencing your own satisfaction or pleasure.

Gratefully Imperfect

So be content with who you are, and don't
put on airs. Live carefree before God.
1 Peter 5:6-7, *THE MESSAGE*

I wanted to be a perfect wife—to be all Richard desired and make him happy that he married me. But my initial goal turned into obsession. I felt compelled to modify my personality, beliefs, talents and hopes to match his. It looked good, but it felt awful.

Eventually, my unrealistic expectations led to burnout. The outward me could no longer live in disharmony with the inner me. I had to do something or crumble. Yet the thought of changing the way Richard and I related to each other scared me.

"What if you don't like me or our marriage when I share the real me?"

"I will," assured my husband.

At first, I didn't believe him. And truthfully, adjusting our conditioned relational patterns—the way we had learned to interact with one another—felt unfamiliar and awkward to us both. Yet gradually we've grown more comfortable sharing our needs, vulnerabilities and desires. We're discovering how to combine who we are on the inside with what we appear to be on the outside. I think we're growing into the individual persons God created us to be. We're also enjoying our imperfect relationship. And I'm grateful.

Lord, please help me to be the person You created me to be.
The me You made is good enough. What a relief.

Make It Personal: In which of your important relationships do you experience difficulty being your imperfectly human self? Consider sharing one uncomfortable reality about yourself to that person. Ask God for courage to be genuine.

Stepping Back
Is Sometimes Best

Jesus replied, "What is impossible
with men is possible with God."

Luke 18:27

I had invited a young mom to have lunch with me, but on the scheduled day, she left a note on my porch, breaking our date. I knew she was having family problems, but I didn't anticipate her message: *I don't think we can be friends. You've never been through anything like this. I can't feel God's help, even though I want to. It's best we not see each other again.*

My immediate response was to reach for the phone to tell her that she had misunderstood. All I wanted to do was be there for her! I wanted to assure her that I had experienced hurtful times, too, and would pray for her and her family. I wanted her to think well of me and of God. If I could just set her straight—lovingly, of course.

But I didn't call. I didn't write. In fact, I didn't even panic. I decided to let God work in my friend's life, unhindered by me. I didn't need the relational crisis to feel valuable. This new behavior wasn't comfortable, but I walked through the unfamiliar feelings and survived.

Positive change is possible.

Lord, I know I can't be everyone's (or anyone's!) savior.
I'd so like to help, yet I realize that stepping back to allow You
and the other person work it out together is sometimes
the best assistance I can give.

Make It Personal: When might stepping back actually allow God and someone you love to work out their solutions together?

Superhero No More

*It is better to take refuge in the Lord
than to trust in man.*

Psalm 118:8

A coworker shared a portion of her recent counseling session with me: "People always expect me to solve everything. I'm tired of trying to be right all the time. When will it end?"

"When you decide you don't want to live this way anymore," said her counselor. "Do you want to stop pretending you're superwoman?"

"No one will want to be with me if I admit I have needs and problems, too," she responded.

"Have I kicked you out yet?" joked the therapist.

"No, but I'm *paying* you."

"It's your decision," repeated her counselor. "Think about your choices. We'll talk again later."

My colleague left with a heavy heart. If she changed her behavior, others would be upset. But another thought bothered her more: *If I stop helping everyone, will it be all right with God?* That week, she explored her options and prayed. Then it dawned on her: *If I continue to play the superhero, I encourage others to trust in me instead of in God. Perhaps if I back off, their faith will have an opportunity to grow.* That day, the weight of the world began to roll off her tired shoulders.

*Lord, I'm beginning to get it: You don't expect me to
be a super-woman or to figure out all the solutions for those
around me. I've allowed others to take advantage.
Please help me establish wise helping patterns.*

Make It Personal: Name an area of your life where you're tempted to play the superhero. Consider deleting one task from your superhero to-do list this week.

Sugarcoated Reality

[Pharaoh] restored the chief cupbearer to his position . . . but he hanged the chief baker, just as Joseph had said to them in his interpretation.

Genesis 40:21-22

A fellow prisoner asked Joseph to help him understand a confusing dream. After acknowledging that God had given him discernment, Joseph interpreted the dream: "You'll be released soon and have your job back."

When another prisoner heard the favorable outcome, he asked Joseph to decode his dream as well. This time, the news wasn't pleasant. Joseph could have massaged the truth to gain a more favorable reaction, but he didn't. His commitment to integrity led him to simply tell the truth (see Genesis 40).

If you're like me, you may have learned to sugarcoat reality. Some of us have been conditioned to believe that we must keep the peace, save another from further disappointment or hedge reality so that someone will feel better.

Yet God is always pleased with the truth. Like Joseph did, we honor integrity when we *do* and *verbalize* on the outside exactly who we *are* on the inside. Practicing integrity allows us to become integrated and complete persons.

Dear Lord, I want to say and do on the outside the same as I think, feel and believe on the inside. Please help me to share the truth, even when it's difficult.

Make It Personal: One of the definitions of the Greek word for "truth" is *the reality right in front of you.* Where have you hedged on the truth (reality) staring you in the face? (Awareness is the first step toward solution.)

Rocking the Boat

If it is possible, as far as it depends on you, live at peace with everyone.

Romans 12:18

As a teen, I hung a copy of this Bible verse inside my locker. I longed to be a peacemaker. Over the ensuing years, becoming a peacemaker began to mean being pleasant and agreeable no matter what the circumstance. It wasn't that I avoided all conflicts with everyone, just primarily with those who meant the most to me. I didn't want them to be upset with me or with the situation.

This desire translated into a "don't rock the boat" mentality. If a bill was due and we had no money to pay it, I hid the truth, taking on the responsibility to work it out. When asked to agree to something I didn't believe was wise, I gave in to maintain peace. If it was inconvenient for me to pursue personal interests, I neglected myself to make another happy.

I thought I was obeying God. I was a peacemaker, wasn't I? I had interpreted the verse to mean, "With all the zeal and drive you can muster, keep the peace." This attitude sabotaged my relationships and contributed to my burnout.

Paul's words in Romans suggest that there are times when peace isn't possible or when peace doesn't depend on us. With God's help, we can become peacemakers without selling our souls to a philosophy of peace at any cost.

Lord, please give me courage to be a truthful peacemaker.

Make It Personal: What does practicing peace at any cost mean to you? Name a time when you courageously refused to give in to this mentality. How did you feel about your action?

Learning to Ask

Ask and it will be given to you.

Luke 11:9

"I'm leaving in the morning on a business trip," said my Bible study partner as she hurried away. "I hope my daughter has my clothes ironed when I get home."

"That would be nice. Did you ask her to help you get things ready?" I asked.

"No, but I'm praying she'll think of it on her own and have it done."

Some of us harbor the misconception that we're selfish to ask directly for what we need or want. We may avoid verbalizing our expectations while unconsciously trying to induce the response we want with silent prayer. This can lead to continual disappointment and a misperception that others don't really understand us or try to meet our needs.

"What do you want from Me?" Jesus asked two blind men. It was a direct question and the men didn't hedge their responses. In fact, they intentionally put themselves in a position to be heard by Jesus. "We want to see," they replied honestly (see Matthew 20:29-34).

Perhaps you've been conditioned to avoid the words *I want*. Maybe you believe that if you have to ask, it ruins everything. Yet Jesus says, "Ask, and it shall be given you." Relating our needs and desires is not unspiritual. God invites us to be up-front with each other and with Him.

Lord, I've sometimes withheld vital information about myself
in the false belief that I'm being more considerate and spiritual.
Please teach me the skills of healthy communication.

Make It Personal: Maybe you neglect to ask directly because you fear the answer. But another's response isn't your responsibility. What will you ask this week?

Joy-filled Honesty

Joy belongs to those who are honest.

Psalm 97:11, *NCV*

When my daughter was about 20 years old, she and I drove to my parents' home in the Midwest. During our visit, Dad asked me to look through my things in storage. As I rummaged through the keepsakes, my eyes fell on a small green book. "Oh, my! I can't believe it!" I exclaimed. "It's my junior high diary!"

Inside of the front cover were the words *SECRET! STAY OUT PLEASE!!!!!* Tiny lettering at the bottom of the page read, "I beg. Ask what it says inside. I'll tell you."

Scanning the messy pages, I cringed. *This girl was immature and boy crazy!* I thought. Upon our return home, I invited my daughter to read it. Several hours later, a surprised young woman walked into my room. "Thanks a lot, Mom, for letting me read your diary. I've always had the feeling you never went through what I did. Like somehow I didn't measure up to what you were in junior high. But you were just like me. Flighty and boy crazy!"

We hugged and laughed. "Actually, it's rather embarrassing," I admitted.

"Well, thanks for allowing me to see a glimpse of that part of your life," she said. "It's like you've validated who I am as a young woman. I feel a sense of relief. I'm grateful and my heart feels lighter." Joy floods our relationships when we interact with openness and loving sincerity.

Lord, help me be open and honest, even before my family.

Make It Personal: In what lighthearted way can and will you share honestly with a loved one during this week?

Healthy Example

Jesus answered, "Peter, before the rooster crows today,
you will deny three times that you know me."
Then Jesus asked them, "When I sent you . . ."

Luke 22:34-35

Although Jesus was fully aware of Peter's upcoming failure, He didn't dwell on it. Neither did Jesus try to maneuver a different response. He told the facts, listened to Peter's reaction and continued with His previous teaching plans. Had I been in charge and experienced Peter's unconcerned response, I probably would have sent Peter on an errand to remove him from the place of temptation!

Jesus didn't let Peter's choices preoccupy His thoughts or detour Him from His own God-given goals. When Jesus walked on this imperfect earth, He didn't choose, think or feel for others what they could choose, think and feel for themselves.

Likewise, we need not spend valuable time trying to control the way others respond to unpleasant information or situations. If the boss is angry when told of a lost account, when a spouse sulks after hearing the car needs repair, when a child doesn't study and fails a class—we needn't panic or strategize to make it better for them. We can learn to stand on our own two feet and let our loved ones do the same. It's a freeing and less exhausting way to interact.

*Lord, I have the opportunity and privilege to choose my
own responses to life's surprises. My friends and family members have
the opportunity to decide for themselves, too. I like that.*

Make It Personal: During the next week, look for other examples of how Jesus interacted with His loved ones.

You Mad at Me?

In God I trust, I will not be afraid. What can man do to me?

Psalm 56:11

"Are you mad at me?" I whispered, after tiptoeing down the steps and into my parents' room. Even when I didn't verbalize the question, I pondered it silently. If they seemed irritated or unhappy, I assumed they were disappointed in me.

When I married, I followed a similar pattern. My "Are you mad at me?" question wasn't always a direct inquiry. Sometimes it was an attitude that permeated the air around me. To prove my love, I thought I must assume or remedy another's sad or angry mood. At times, I believed that I was the *cause* of my loved one's unhappiness or distress.

But I've changed and I'm amazed—though admittedly imperfect. (Hey, that's one reason I'm so amazed!) I'm not as afraid of the reactions of those I love. When my husband or best friend has a bad day or doesn't like something I've done, it doesn't automatically ruin my day; I don't automatically forgo my sense of personal wellbeing.

Usually I can say with the psalmist, "What can man do to me? I will rely on God and not be afraid." This new mindset releases me from my former prison of fear. And I'm incredibly grateful.

*God, I want to stop worrying about a loved
one's response to life or to me. So today I put my confidence
in You—and there find relief.*

Make It Personal: The next time a loved one is in a bad mood and you feel the urge to "take it on," step back emotionally and ask God for wisdom.

Ultimate Paradox

Whoever loses his life for my sake will find it.

Matthew 10:39

"Lord, I can't guarantee my husband's reactions and beliefs," I prayed. "I'm tired of trying. I release him." I considered the implications and continued, "I can't predict the future; he may choose to leave. Yet I can't keep trying so hard to do what isn't my responsibility anyway. I give up control of his life and mine. The result is Yours."

Reflecting on my decision, I'm at a loss to effectively share it. I faced the end of my trying so hard to make it all just right in this relationship that meant so much to me. I couldn't change Richard to better understand me or God, so I accepted my powerlessness and unleashed my hold. This involved a level of faith I hadn't experienced before: trusting that surrender was wise, that the process would be worthwhile and that God was in complete control whatever the result.

It seemed like the ultimate paradox: In order to find what was missing (reduced fear, joy, rest from over-trying and over-caring, God's unconditional love), I released what I longed for (nurturing relationship, increased intimacy, healthy interaction, mutual validation).

In his book *Inside Out*, Larry Crabb describes the surrendering process this way: "As we walk a path that seems to lead toward death, a sense of life quietly grows within us."[18] I let go, not into the unknown space, but into the hands of a personal God.

Lord, I release the grip I have on my world.
In exchange, I regain life.

Make It Personal: What (or whom) do you need to let go of? Consider what this might mean.

Speaking the Truth in Love

Speaking the truth in love.

Ephesians 4:15

If you don't have something nice to say, say nothing at all. I heard this advice at church, school and home. So I made it my creed.

But it's a half-truth. For example, Paul writes, "Be kind and loving to each other" (Ephesians 4:32, *NCV*). When we act on this truth, our relationships flourish. Yet sometimes we need to tell our children or our nieces and nephews what they don't want to hear. "Don't play in the street" or "Be home by midnight" or "No, you can't wear that outfit to school" doesn't seem *nice* to them. Speaking the painful truth to a parent or spouse is even harder. "No, I won't lie to your boss" or "I don't like it when you yell at me" or "Your driving is endangering lives" may be met with rejection.

In *Telling Each Other the Truth*, William Backus writes, "We cannot measure love solely by whether or not what we say hurts someone's feelings. The fact that another person may not like what we have spoken does not automatically mean we have done wrong."[19]

It may be difficult for those of us who try hard to think, do and say the *right* thing to speak the truth in love. But God promises us courage. He will help us through the rough spots.

Lord, help me not to merely say what people want to hear or try to pacify others by telling half-truths. Although it feels uncomfortable, I do want to be lovingly honest in my relationships.

Make It Personal: What are you tolerating because you're trying to be nice? Ask God to help you find a way to "speak the truth in love."

Lonely Lovers Song

Your love is better than life.

Psalm 63:3

"What makes Psalm 63 special to so many people?" asked my Bible study leader.

From the corner of the room, a quiet voice responded, "It's a song for lonely lovers. It's *my* psalm."

This answer surprised everyone. On the surface, it seemed unspiritual, but was it?

Feeling love is often difficult for those of us whose mothers, fathers, husbands or friends haven't been there for us emotionally or physically. We may feel abandoned, used, unwanted or loved conditionally. Longing for the acceptance inherent in genuine love, we identify with poet David in this psalm.

We're frustrated lovers. And according to the women I've spent hours coaching and mentoring, it doesn't matter whether we're married or not. We all experience lonely moments looking and longing for intimacy. Human love can be both wonderful *and* disappointing. It will never be perfectly engaging and fulfilling all the time. Only God is flawless, and being confident of His love is better than life.

O God, I agree with David. Experiencing Your acceptance and understanding love is better than life itself. In the midst of my imperfect human relationships, my heart longs for You. You give my spirit a refreshing drink of unconditional love. Alone at night, I think of You. Your unshaming presence brings a song to my lips. You never push me away, so my heart clings to You. You are stronger and more stable than I. You fulfill my deep, insatiable longing for love. I am grateful.

Make It Personal: Read the 11 verses of Psalm 63 and circle the words or phrases that speak most to you.

Healthy Rescuing

He is the living God and he endures forever; He rescues and he saves.
Daniel 6:26-27

While scanning our local newspaper, I read the true stories of a lifeguard who saved a toddler from drowning, a nurse who performed CPR on a heart-attack patient, and a passing motorist who interceded for an elderly mugging victim. These caring individuals stepped in to save another from danger or death when the victims could not help themselves. These accounts illustrate a beneficial kind of rescuing.

Yet some of us have pushed our helping attempts over the line into unhealthy rescuing, perhaps in part because we espouse one or all of the following untruths: (1) Other people are incapable of helping themselves adequately, so I must do it for them; (2) I should try to fix or change someone when he/she is sad, disappointed or angry; (3) It is my personal responsibility to keep all things on an even keel for my family and friends; and (4) I am responsible for my family members' happiness and satisfaction. My contentment depends on theirs.

Unnecessary rescuing can preoccupy our thoughts, deplete our energy and keep us from spending time developing our own God-given gifts. We just don't have the time to do it all. Yet, there's space, breath and relief when we debunk the lies and leave the saving and rescuing to our tireless and compassionate God.

*Lord, teach me the difference between healthy
and unhealthy helping. I'm really tired.*

Make It Personal: Think of a time when you suspected someone was trying to rescue you because they thought you couldn't do it yourself. What did it feel like?

Breaking and Entering

If we confess our sins, he is faithful and just and will forgive us our sins and purify us from all unrighteousness.

1 John 1:9

"With God's help, I'm learning to love again," said my Bible study partner. "Somewhere along the line, I learned that loving another person means getting inside his skin; trying to make him a better person, attempting to influence his decisions, pushing him toward maturity. Now I realize healthy love means standing alongside, supporting, accepting and validating the other's thoughts and emotions. It's a less demanding take on love and quite unfamiliar to me. I need daily help staying committed to loving this way."

I identify. When I began to grasp this truth about love, God showed me that trying to get inside another's thoughts or feelings in order to alter reactions and behavior is "breaking and entering." It's against God's moral and spiritual law. When I attempt to climb inside and change another's beliefs, emotions or perceptions to either match my own or become what I think they *should* be, I impersonate the Holy Spirit. Once I understood this, I felt sad and genuinely remorseful.

So I ran to God, my gracious and understanding Father. I admitted my shortcomings and sins, and He splashed me with forgiveness and joy.

Lord, I've committed "breaking and entering"
crimes against others and against You. Thank You for
forgiving me. Help me forgive myself.

Make It Personal: What do you need from God? Share your heart. Write and date your prayer here or in your journal so that you can read it later and find strength to stay committed to positive change.

Beneficial Detachment

Lord . . . I don't pretend to "know it all." I am quiet now before
the Lord . . . . Yes, my begging has been stilled.

Psalm 131:1-2, *TLB*

Once a month, Mary and I met to have breakfast and chat. One particular morning Mary shared, "My son-in-law walked out on my daughter and grandchildren. Must be a mid-life crisis. He doesn't make any sense. I've been trying to figure it out, but it's so confusing."

"You okay?" I asked.

"He's driving me crazy," Mary responded. "I need to get through to him. He's making a huge mistake."

Mary looked like she hadn't slept. Detaching from her son-in-law's erratic behavior might have helped her deal with her family's loss, but it was hard for her to let go. She so wanted him to realize his wrong and come back to his wife and children. Although that appeared to be the sensible solution, the more she tried to make it happen, the less likely it became.

Several months later at our early-morning get-together, she said, "I can't change him, as much as I want to. So I've pulled away from trying to fix him or that marriage. I hope doing so will make room for God to heal. I do know it has restored my peace of mind—and that's been good. I'm sleeping better."

Lord, detaching does not mean I don't
care anymore. I care a great deal, but I know
I can't fix what another has broken. You are the Master
Repairman. I'll let You do Your job.

Make It Personal: In what way would detaching from someone else's problem benefit you?

First Things First

Why do you look at the speck of sawdust in your brother's eye
and pay no attention to the plank in your own eye?

Luke 6:41

"Why didn't you tell me the contractor called to change an installation date?" I asked. "Now I've missed the deadline."

"Well, you're so busy," explained my assistant. "I was trying to save you from more stress." (She could have added, "And keep you from being so demanding.")

I understand both sides of this story. *Protectors*, like my talented assistant, become expert at hiding the unpleasant truth from others (for their own good, of course). *Intimidators*, like the harried boss (that's me, unfortunately!), get so focused on achieving goals that we unintentionally push people away. While wanting to make everything just right, we both could easily discern the errors in the other's actions. Sadly, we each remained unaware of our own troubling behavior.

Jesus addressed this situation when He said, "First, deal with your own need (the plank in your eye!); then you can help another." In fact, the most beneficial thing we can do for our children, colleagues and friends is to deal honestly with our own problems, whether they are over-caring, workaholism or other issues that contribute to our intimidating and protecting personas. If we wish to favorably influence others, we will confront our own perfectionistic problems and commit to positive personal change. Coming to God with expectancy and faith will help us understand ourselves and experience self-worth.

Lord, help me to see myself clearly. I want to
offer the greater gift: a healthy example.

Make It Personal: When have you been a healthy example of positive change?

Playing God

Carry each other's burdens, and in this way you will fulfill the law
of Christ. . . . Each one should test his own actions. Then he
can take pride in himself, without comparing himself
to somebody else, for each one should carry his own load.

Galatians 6:2-5

When I memorized these verses, I felt confused. *I can and will carry others' burdens,* I agreed, *but how can I be so selfish as to be concerned with my own problems? My major consideration should be for other people and their troubles.* My understanding of these verses contributed to an over-active sense of responsibility and eventual burnout. I believed that I was obeying God by helping others while neglecting myself.

I've since learned what Paul, the author of Galatians, knew all along: I rob myself and others if I assume their daily problems or needs. When I do for others what they can do for themselves, I keep them from learning life skills and gaining the resulting self-respect. By trying to carry all the burdens, I play God.

Most people need assistance during times of excessive difficulty, and we're privileged to help. Yet when we take responsibility for another's day-to-day dilemmas, we're headed for disappointment. And chronic disappointment often leads to disillusionment and exhaustion. This isn't the way to fulfill Christ's directives. We need not carry more than our share of everyday loads. Isn't this great news?

Lord, please help me make prudent decisions
about how and when to help.

Make It Personal: Make a list of appropriate times to help someone with a heavy burden. Then make a list of everyday loads that aren't your responsibility.

Jesus' Boundaries

And having sent them away, he got in
the boat with his disciples.

Mark 8:9-10

"We've been here for a long time now," said Jesus to His disciples. "Some of these families have traveled far. I feel for them. They may faint from hunger on the way home. Let's give them something to eat" (see Mark 8:1-10). So Jesus fed 4,000 men and their families, who ate until they were satisfied.

Then Jesus sent them away. He left with His disciples. Perhaps some in the crowd begged Him to stay. Maybe some thought He would provide a place to spend the night and make them breakfast in the morning. But Jesus called a halt to the teaching, broke up the gathering and sailed away. He patiently taught the crowds and graciously provided a miraculous banquet, but that didn't prevent Him from setting a time limit and drawing a firm boundary on His generosity.

"We don't have to be willing to lose everything for love. In fact, setting and sticking to reasonable, healthy limits in all our relationships is a prerequisite to love and relationships that work. We can learn to make appropriate choices concerning what we're willing to *give* in our relationships—of ourselves, time, talents and money," writes Melody Beattie in her book *Beyond Codependency*.[20]

Although we might think love is always giving and fulfilling someone else's needs, by observing Jesus' example we learn that we can love and still set limits.

Lord, teach me about both sides of genuine love.
I want to learn to give and take.

Make It Personal: Remember a recent time when you experienced loving "give and take" in a significant relationship. What did you like about that?

Win-Win Listening

Always be willing to listen and slow to speak.

James 1:19, *NCV*

"As I gave my friend a copy of *The Relief of Imperfection*, I shared my personal story [included in the book] with her," emailed a colleague. "I can't explain how healing that was for me. I felt safe enough to share the hurts of my career and marriage. She didn't judge me; instead, she listened and affirmed the positive changes I've made. This opened the door for us to grow our friendship without trying to fix one another. At times, we just chuckle at our exasperating life circumstances and sigh with relief: We don't have to try so hard to make ourselves *just right*."

Listening is a win-win for relationships because it validates the one being listened to while it lowers the listener's urgency to appear knowledgeable, wise or repair a behavior or situation. Although listening without advising may feel uncomfortable at first (because it's generally an unfamiliar way to relate in our society), after a little practice, it offers loads of relief—to *everyone*.

Lord, please help me listen with Your love.

Make It Personal: Consider playing the Listening Game with a partner. Read one to three devotions together or privately. One shares her response to the story or Make It Personal question/suggestion. The other listens for two minutes without commenting (no advice, Scripture verses or "I did that, too!" remarks). Smiles and eye contact are fine. Then switch so the first listener shares her responses to the devotion/questions while the other listens without talking.

What was it like to listen without commenting? What was it like to be listened to without interruption?

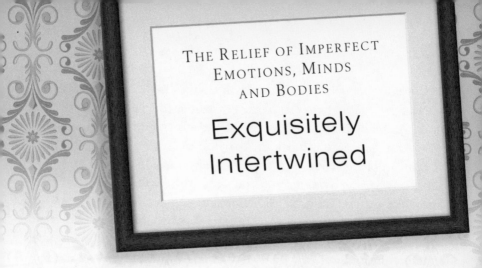

Exquisitely Intertwined

I mentioned to my doctor that I wrote a book titled *The Relief of Imperfection: For Women Who Try Too Hard to Make It Just Right* and he smirked (that's how it looked to me). As I walked out, he shouted down the hall, "Is it an autobiography?"

I stuttered, "Uh, no-o-o." It surprised me how miffed I felt. *Humph. How dare he?* Reminds me of when a physical therapist tried to help me relax, so he hooked me to a biofeedback machine. He left the room and my pulse quickened and my neck tensed (I tried hard to keep that from happening!). The machine's meter jerked wildly. *Someone's messing with it from the adjoining room*, I surmised. He returned and removed the wires from me. "Guess we'll forget this," he said.

I had a difficult time chilling out. I write this embarrassing episode to illustrate a point: Everything about us is exquisitely designed and intertwined. The mind affects the emotions (and vice-versa). Emotions affect the body. What happens in the body affects your personality *and* actions—even when you don't want it to.

I joke about it, but this topic of imperfect emotions, minds and bodies intimidates me. Besides being deeply personal, it's massive. Under this subject's lid simmers a stew of sub-issues including body image, dieting, exercise, nutrition, hormones, disabilities, anorexia, bulimia, overeating, PMS, peri- and post-menopause, pregnancy, post-partum, anxiety, abortion, depression, denial, malaise, inferiority, shame, addictions, self-esteem, mental illness, grief, aging, abuse, counseling, physical therapy, codependency, and other publicized problems and possible solutions. (Do you get the picture?)

In childhood I acquired nicknames like "Perfecto" and "Martyr," yet I assure you that I'm just like other people: touched by imperfection and personally humbled by some of the aforementioned experiences, including depression, burnout, body-image issues, PMS and menopausal problems, codependency, spousal obsession, weight loss gone haywire, sleep deprivation, antidepressant withdrawal, an anorexic teenage daughter, and multiple addictions of extended family.

Over the years, I got the impression that I should keep a lid on all this—and that it's ungodly to admit to emotions like disappointment, sadness, anger, discouragement and bewilderment. But that's a misconception. Although maintaining a positive outlook is worthwhile, you and I needn't pretend that we never hurt or make mistakes. King David didn't, and God called him a "man after My own heart" (see 1 Samuel 13:14). I know that not everyone tends to withhold their emotions as I do. Perhaps you feel that you *must* verbalize and release your emotions or you'll explode. Short-tempered displays, sideways sarcasm or shaming attempts to control may get you in a pickle just as hiding does for me.

Yet God loves and cares for us both. He wants us to live harmoniously with our emotions, thoughts and unique body shapes. So grab courage and get the help you need, despite how uneasy it makes you or others feel. Ask questions. Share with a kind listener. See a competent doctor or counselor—and if you don't connect with the first one, try another. Just start the process. Jesus took care of Himself (see Matthew 12:14-15). So can you.

In fact, the wisdom manual (Proverbs) indicates that your greatest responsibility is to protect and nurture your soul, which houses with your unique mind, feelings and personality. So guard your inner self, because out of it flows your entire life—everything you are (see Proverbs 4:23). The most beneficial thing you and I can do for our children, colleagues, friends and loved ones is deal honestly with our own self-image issues, vacillating emotions and misconceptions. God graciously gives us the privilege of making positive changes and developing spiritual, mental, physical and emotional muscle. You and I don't have to be perfect to be loving, healthy and committed Christian women. I love that, don't you?

Accepting My Humanness

[Jesus] was crucified in weakness, yet he lives by God's power.
Likewise, we are weak in him, yet by God's power we will live.

2 Corinthians 13:4

"I hate weakness," I admitted in a rare inactive moment. I had accepted a coworker's lunch invitation—unusual, since I didn't eat lunch unless it was a business meeting. So what prompted this verbal disclosure? I was exasperated by management's inability to dismiss an employee after we had all agreed that it was necessary, though regrettable.

Other people's lack of commitment to hard work irritated me; no one else stayed until 9:00 P.M. to get projects completed! Also, my decreasing stamina concerned me. Recognizing weakness (actually, humanness) in another person reminded me of my own fallibility, and I didn't like feeling needy, imperfect or tired. So I gave myself an anti-weakness pep talk: *You can do it, Joan. Just try harder.*

I disliked my human emotions, frailties and limitations, so I often pretended that they didn't exist. As I write this now, I chuckle at my audacity. Even Jesus (God's Son in the flesh) lived with human restrictions. He, too, was limited by time, space, hunger, exhaustion and a human body.

It took time to begin accepting my humanness. It's an ongoing process for me. Yet because Christ lived on this imperfect earth, He understands my frustration. By the power of Jesus' death and resurrection, I experience God working in my human weakness—and that's both soothing and energizing to me.

Lord, I'm a limited human being living in an imperfect world.
Thanks for Your power working in my weakness.

Make It Personal: When have you noticed God's power working in your humanness?

Calm When I Goof

Calmness can lay great errors to rest.

Ecclesiastes 10:4

As I left the store, I noticed a flashing red light in the parking lot. Soon I realized the police were prying into my car with a coat hanger. Racing to the scene I asked, "What's the problem?"

"This your car?" shouted one policeman, ignoring my question. "You didn't put it in park," accused the other officer. "It rolled back and creamed this van. Besides that, you left your lights on!"

Shame on you, Joan, I scolded silently. *How stupid! I didn't want to run this errand for my husband anyway.* Then I caught myself. *Okay. It isn't my husband's fault. I made a mistake. I wish I had put the car in park and turned off the lights, but I'm human and I goofed.*

I drove my car forward in response to the officer's directions. Thanks to sufficient safety bumpers, neither vehicle incurred any damage. The policemen smiled sheepishly.

Sometimes I panic and first resort to belittling myself (or others) when I'm faced with a problem or crisis. Perhaps you've experienced this as well. The good news is that with practice, you and I can learn to release our shaming and blaming tendencies and respond in new—and relaxed—ways to each day's diverse situations and unique mistakes. Relief follows.

Lord, help me break my old habit of
shaming and blaming. I want to practice calm
when I goof up. I need Your help.

Make It Personal: When's the last time you goofed? How did you react? Given an opportunity to respond again, what would you do differently?

Flashlight of Hope

So overflowing is his kindness towards us that he took away all
our sins through the blood of his Son . . . and he has
showered down upon us the richness of his grace.

Ephesians 1:7, *TLB*

"Listen to this," gushed our facilitator. "While preparing for this lesson in Ephesians, I noticed the words *rich* and *riches* are mentioned six times. God promises us abundance and fullness because of Christ's gift on the cross. That's exciting to me. What's your reaction?"

"To tell you the truth, I don't feel rich," I (a pastor's wife) said. "I feel like I'm walking in darkness—empty."

Silence filled the room. None of the other pastors' wives and women's leaders knew how to respond. I no longer remember how our small group resumed that evening. What I do recall is how my surprising revelation broke open a crack in the "everything's fine" wall I had built around myself, providing a positive first step out of my depression. The truth was out. Now I could seek help and pray for God's specific intervention.

I risked sharing my real feelings and thoughts with trustworthy friends and it allowed a little flashlight of hope to pierce my darkness. Several others gained the courage to voice their reality, as well. By taking one tiny step away from the painful isolation, we moved toward purpose and healing.

*Lord, because of Your grace, I want to be authentic with the caring
people You put into my life. It's scary. Please help me.*

Make It Personal: Where are you pretending "everything's fine"? Consider sharing your feelings and thoughts with a compassionate friend who will listen without offering solutions.

Precious to God

"Look at the birds of the air; they do not sow or reap or store
away in barns, and yet your heavenly Father feeds them.
Are you not much more valuable that they?"

Matthew 6:26

I took a break from writing to accompany my husband, Richard, on a business trip to California's Half Moon Bay. From our room, I gazed at an amazing view below: crashing ocean waves, dark rock cliffs, multi-colored gardens surrounding a gazebo and the lush eighteenth fairway, all nestled against an azure backdrop interspersed with billowing clouds.

The bellman said, "Enjoy now. It'll rain soon." He raised the window only four inches because there were no screens. A welcome breeze caressed my face as I plopped on the bed to relax. Dozing in and out of sleep, I opened my eyes to a big black bird, staring me down and ready to pounce.

"Richard!" I screamed. The bird turned, hopped over the bed to the window seat and flew out the small window opening—just as if he'd done this before and knew exactly how to escape another screeching woman!

Later I recalled the words of Matthew 6:26. That audacious little (relatively speaking!) bird *and* all the other fowl in the air never worry, count calories or try to win favor, yet God sees and provides for them. And here's the amazing part: You and I mean much more to God than soaring or snoopy birds.

Lord, how grateful I am that You
value me even though I don't have a perfect
body or faultless emotions.

Make It Personal: How has God shown you lately that you're precious to Him?

Blinking in Amazement

*Whatsoever things are true . . . honest . . . just . . . pure . . .
lovely . . . of good report, if there be any virtue, and . . .
any praise, think on these things.*

Philippians 4:8

I believed that to be a loving Christian woman, I must pretend that I didn't mind being taken advantage of or mistreated. I ignored any painful matters. (Didn't this verse mean that I should think only about lovely, pure things?) Because I couldn't allow myself to think about anything uncomfortable, I didn't acknowledge that change was necessary. Neither could I pray specifically about what concerned or hurt me (see Philippians 4:6).

Then I learned that one of the original meanings of the Greek word for "truth" is *the reality clearly lying before your eyes.*[21] I blinked in amazement. Indeed I *could* admit unpleasantness.

I've met many women who have remained stuck, unable to live out God's design for them because they believe they can't (as godly women) acknowledge or talk about any hurtful reality, whether it's abuse, addiction, depression, eating disorders, post-partum or menopausal problems, anger or grief. I've also met women—just like me—who've courageously confronted their uncomfortable reality, knowing that there is virtue in honestly growing through the pain to dwell on the true, just, pure and lovely things God has for them.

*Lord, help me admit the truth,
whether delightful or disagreeable.*

Make It Personal: List what is good about your life in one column, what concerns or perplexes you in another column and what hurts you in a third column. Bring the three-columned list before God, asking for guidance in dealing with your reality.

Just for Today

O Lord, be gracious to us; we long for you.
Be our strength every morning.

Isaiah 33:2

Can I learn to live with my inconsistent and ambivalent feelings, thoughts and behaviors? I am so imperfect, jerked back and forth between benevolence and self-preoccupation, wandering aimlessly between restlessness and peace. I long to believe God completely, but I wobble.

I awakened this morning with a song about Jesus playing in my mind (a God-gift, certainly!). Journaling my gratefulness, I drew musical notes on the page. Yet last night I went to sleep with an upset stomach, headache and nose so congested that my CPAP mask (for treating sleep apnea[22]) didn't work. I sighed: *Lord God, my heart is heavy. Such sadness surrounds those I love. And I'm supposed to be writing a relief-producing book here.*

I admit that I'm rarely satisfied. I want more faith, growth, insight, consistency, harmony, love. Will I ever have enough? Probably not.

Can I come to terms with this? I want to. But how? I'm compelled to think and feel *just right*. Dr. David Stoop, author of *Living with a Perfectionist*, suggests facing the lifelong challenge of accepting my humanness "one day at a time. This means that each day is the only part of the process [I] can see and affect, so [I'm] satisfied with growth that comes in small steps."[23] So, just for today, I'll release what cannot be, breathing deeply and appreciating what I have. Just for today.

Lord, one morning at a time I wait for You.
You are my strength for renewal and change.

Make It Personal: What will you do "just for today" that you can't guarantee tomorrow?

Agreeing with My Maker

Woe to him who quarrels with his Maker . . . Does the clay say to the potter, "What are you making?" Does your work say, "He has no hands"?

Isaiah 45:9

I asked a lovely young mother how she handles residual emotions and thoughts from former anorexic days. She shared:

> Sometimes I wonder why I'm shaped like I am, or feel sad about the parts of my body I dislike, or covet how another woman is formed, thinking she looks better than I do. Then I find help in Isaiah 45:9 and Psalm 139:13-18. God planned how I'd look—the parts I think are beautiful and the parts I don't. I'm not my body only; however, my body is part of who I am and is crafted by the same God who fashioned my soul—strengths, talents, passions and limitations.

I identify. I don't want to bicker with my loving Maker, either. Yet I have at times. The word "woe" in Isaiah 45:9 appears to be a Hebrew exclamation for expressing pain or grief. Interesting; that's how I feel when I compare myself and my body to unreasonable standards or to someone else (*she* probably likes what I don't!). God intends to spare me the painful isolation I experience when I question His plans for me.

I think I'll take another step toward accepting my obvious aging process!

Gradual growth is okay with God. He doesn't shame me for having incredibly human thoughts and emotions about myself. What an amazing God I love.

Lord, I feel close to You right now.
Thanks for creating me.

Make It Personal: Read Psalm 139:13-18. Circle words that draw you to God.

It's an Epidemic

You made [mankind] . . . and crowned him
with glory and honor.

Psalm 8:5

There's an epidemic of body dissatisfaction in our homes, schools, churches and world. Why else would nearly every magazine flash articles on dieting, exercise and makeovers in every issue? The search for "body perfectdom" sometimes leads to an eating disorder such as anorexia, bulimia or EDNOS (Eating Disorder Not Otherwise Specified).[24] Records show that in the United States alone, 10 million women and girls suffer from anorexia and bulimia, and 25 million more from EDNOS.[25]

I read (in one of those magazines) about a well-known person who acknowledges that her childhood experiences contributed to an erroneous body image in her adult life. She's now working toward accepting her human body, integrating the past with reality and not being ashamed anymore. I respect that.

As human beings, we are created in the image of God (see Genesis 1:27) and crowned with glory and honor. The human body, with its obvious limitations, became the dignified dwelling for God incarnate (see John 1:14). As this truth slowly penetrates my mind and emotions, I gain increased permission to relax with my current appearance, do the best with what I have and accept what will not change. I admit that this isn't always easy, yet I've chosen to partner with God in this personal growth area—as well as in the more spiritually sounding ones. It's an imperfect journey that I'll be on until I walk into the arms of Jesus in heaven.

Lord, help me accept the body that houses
my God-given personality and spirit.

Make It Personal: How does the epidemic of body dissatisfaction impact you?

Like a Refreshing Breeze

The fruit of the Spirit is love, joy, peace, patience, kindness, goodness, faithfulness, gentleness and self-control.

Galatians 5:22-23

"What specific quality would you like for God to develop in you this year?" asked the speaker. It was the first week of January, and we were all contemplating our annual goals. This question caught my attention and wouldn't let go.

Driving home, I contemplated my response: *I'd like to be less obsessive, less intense. I want to balance giving with receiving and then be comfortable with it. I want to learn to accept the person God designed me to be. I want to be less judgmental of myself and others.*

Then a light bulb flashed in my mind: *Gentleness! That's what I want. I want to be more gentle.*

Later, I looked up the word "gentle" and read this definition: "Kindly; moderate; a mild breeze, usually one with the velocity of no more than 12 miles per hour."[26] I smiled as I imagined going through each day at a moderate pace. After all, I had previously run through life like a high-velocity wind, all while trying to keep my emotions and thoughts controlled. Now I desired gentleness.

I shared my goal with God, asked for His Spirit's help and kept this picture in my mind and heart: Joan practicing gentleness, tenderness and kindness, first with herself and then touching others like a refreshing gentle breeze.

Lord, what specific characteristic do we
want to develop in me right now?

Make It Personal: Talk with God about your desire and draw a mental picture of what it will look like when you develop this quality in your life.

Admitting Anger

Then the LORD said . . . "Why are you angry? . . ."
So Cain went out from the LORD's presence.

Genesis 4:6,16

After my perfectionism-induced burnout, I began to honestly verbalize my thoughts, only to experience uncomfortable emotions. My anger scared me. Then I read Cain's story.

"Cain, why are you angry?" God asked. He tried to interact with Cain about what was happening inside him, but Cain ignored God. Sadly, Cain's anger turned to rage and murder. In amazement, I realized that God didn't want Cain to pretend he wasn't angry. Instead, God gave Cain the opportunity to talk about his bitterness—but Cain chose to disregard God's offer of help.

What impressed me was that God moved *toward* Cain even though God knew Cain's angry thoughts and emotions. In his book *Codependency*, Pat Springle writes, "In the unconditional love and acceptance of God, we have an environment in which we can be honest. We not only can acknowledge our present hurt and anger, but we can be objective about the cumulative hurts of the past—and the resulting anger that has been stored inside us."[27]

Although I previously believed otherwise, I now realize that admitting my anger is the first step in dealing constructively with this repressed emotion that once made me sick. What a relief it is to be able to express my feelings without being shamed or dismissed. God's love makes it possible.

Dear God, feeling my anger is a new
experience for me. Please help me to admit it
and deal with it in healthy ways.

Make It Personal: What do you resent? Ponder telling God and another non-judgmental person.

Reducing Resentment

And the Lord's servant must . . .
be kind . . . not resentful.

2 Timothy 2:24

When I started feeling my anger, I was shocked. Since I believed a godly woman shouldn't have this negative emotion, I needed to deny it or call it something else. (What? Maybe selfishness.)

Yet as I became healthier emotionally, I learned that anger is a normal human response to inequity, injustice or wrong, and that it doesn't automatically erupt in uncontrollable rage. I also discovered that it's not wise to continually suppress displeasure, because unresolved anger often turns into resentment. Built-up resentment gets shoved into the body, causing problems and robbing peace. I don't want to be a resentful person, so I seek ways to decrease my susceptibility to anger and resentment and take responsibility for my emotions and actions. It helps when I:

- Make my own choices, taking charge of my personal schedule.
- Say no as well as yes.
- Stay true to my own beliefs and values, regardless of those who differ with me.
- Set and accept reasonable limits.
- Stop trying to manage what isn't mine to control.
- Adjust the misconceptions I have about anger.
- Ask questions when I need clarification.
- Respectfully confront injustice or wrong.
- Pray and trust God before, during and after I've done all I can do.
- Remember that only God is flawless and no one or nothing else is perfect.

Lord, I want to love and serve You and others without resentment.

Make It Personal: Consider choosing one of the above resentment-reducing actions to implement this week.

Internal Friends

*Because of the sacrifice of the Messiah . . . we're a free people—
free of penalties and punishments chalked up by all our misdeeds.*

Ephesians 1:17, *THE MESSAGE*

I emailed a life coaching partner to ask if she would share her story. Yesterday, she replied:

> They said I'd be "just fine." I wasn't. Every day I thought about the child I aborted and what life would have been like with her/him. Guilt, anguish and self-hatred were my unhealthy internal friends. I continually wondered when I'd make the next big mistake. This kept me from taking positive risks with family, friends, and at work. For over twenty years I doubted life would ever be wonderful.
>
> Although I asked Jesus for forgiveness, I couldn't accept His forgiveness or forgive my husband or myself for making *that* decision. Nearing the end of my current career, I worked with a Christian life coach to plan my next career—perhaps in ministry. Yet it became clear to me that I needed healing. Taking a huge risk, I sought help through a God-centered abortion healing program.[28] While walking with a mentor through the process, I found the relief I longed for: God *does* love and forgive me; I *can* and *did* forgive myself and my husband—and I'll see my baby in heaven [see 2 Samuel 12:22-23]. I thought I'd never live without nagging shame. Yet here's what happened: My internal unhealthy friends moved out and I now enjoy a new friendship with hope, faith and joy.

Lord, thanks for freeing me.

Make It Personal: Name your internal healthy and unhealthy friends. Which friendship will you nurture? What do you need to help you do so?

Ignoring Reality

He will wipe every tear from their eyes. There will be no more death
or mourning or crying or pain.

Revelation 21:4

While attending a personal-growth workshop, I completed a question-
naire concerning the developmental tasks of adulthood. After acknowledging my roles as wife, mother, daughter, sister, friend, writer and
child of God, I contemplated my childhood, marriage and babies, career shifts, and dreams lost. When I factored in the inherent adjust-
ments involved in coping with loss, aging, relationships, illness and
inevitable disappointments, I suddenly exclaimed, "It's a lie! Life is not
simple! I've been fed a lie!"

"Life is difficult," wrote M. Scott Peck in his classic bestseller *The
Road Less Traveled.* "This . . . is a great truth because once we truly see
this truth, we transcend it. . . . Once it is accepted, the fact that life is
difficult no longer matters."[29] I'd never really understood what he
meant, but suddenly it made sense.

As long as I could be convinced that life is simple and requires little
work, I ignored reality, asked few questions and rarely complained. It
may have made things "easier" for those around me, but it left me feeling confused and marginalized. Yet once I admitted that life is complex,
I began to relax and cease the silent demand that imperfection go away.

*Lord, someday all the pain and confusion
will cease. Until then, I'll admit that life is often difficult and
stop trying to appear so perfect.*

Make It Personal: When do you ignore reality? How is that working
for you?

A Healthy Habit

As Jesus was getting into the boat, the man who had
been demon-possessed begged to go with him. Jesus did
not let him, but said, "Go home to your family and
tell them how much the Lord has done for you."

Mark 5:18-19

For years, I avoided using the word "no." Sometimes doing so meant that I participated in situations I felt were contrary to God's plan for me. Often it meant that I hid my thoughts or feelings when they differed from someone else's. I neglected my own physical and spiritual needs for rest, because I believed I couldn't refuse others' requests and still be a loving wife, friend and coworker. I felt used and burned up.

Eventually, I realized that I could no longer function effectively by always giving in. I noticed that Jesus said no when He thought it was beneficial, like when He refused the newly healed man's request and sent him home instead.

I began to say no at appropriate times. At first, it felt extremely unfamiliar and uncomfortable, but in time I developed a healthy habit. One of my journal entries indicates my progress. I wrote: "No, no, no, no, no." In fact, the word "no" filled the page. The last line read: "AND IT'S OKAY!" Musical notes lined the margins. I am singing a new song.

*Lord, help me to have the courage to say no when I believe
it is sensible to do so. I want to follow Your example.*

Make It Personal: If you have trouble saying no, I challenge you to say no 15 times this week. *No?* Okay, that's your first one. Only 14 more to go!

Spiritual Tug-of-War

*Since an overseer is entrusted with God's work,
he must be . . . self-controlled.*

Titus 1:7-8

Yesterday, I talked to a talented single woman from the West Coast who said, "I feel like I'm in a tug-of-war. My longing for love and acceptance and my disappointed feelings and thoughts yank me from one side, and what I know I *should* believe about God and Scripture pull on my other arm. I'm caught in the middle and I'm just plain exhausted."

I identify. Some of us have the mistaken idea that in order to be effective Christian women, we must shame ourselves into superior spiritual form. Sadly, sometimes we use Scripture to beat ourselves into shape—or as we'd rather view it, make us self-controlled. In the quest to become spiritually mature, at times we treat ourselves poorly, with accusations like "You don't trust God enough" or "You shouldn't feel sad" or "You—lazy! Get with it" or "God expects more of you."

Yet Jesus calls us to rest, not to exhaustion (see Matthew 11:28-30), so let's adjust our definition of self-control. Although we're responsible for our behavior, thoughts and growth, we need not whip ourselves into action. Positive reinforcement is more helpful. Today, ask: *What do I need to support and help myself?* The answer may surprise you. Maybe you need a hug, a break, a word of encouragement, a visit with a friend or forgiveness. We cultivate self-control by being firm but gentle; honest yet kind; and fair but understanding.

*Lord, I want to stop shaming myself. Please help
me practice positive self-management.*

Make It Personal: If you feel caught in a spiritual tug-of-war, visualize dropping your arms. What happens next?

Forever Friends

A friend loves at all times.

Proverbs 17:17

I'm happy to say that I've renewed a lost friendship. The friendship is with *me*. I've learned to listen to myself, to affirm my perceptions and emotions. I even laugh at myself sometimes, feeling less threatened. On my collision course toward burnout, I felt angry at the person I had become. I treated myself poorly. But now I genuinely want what is best for me, just as I do for my other friends. I'm learning to allow myself space to recuperate when I'm tired or tense (evidenced by the fact that I just took a break—my brain was turning mushy—to walk over the hill to the Llama Ranch I kept hearing about—fun!). When I blow it, I let myself feel the annoyance and then move quickly to forgive myself. (Usually!)

I realize that I'll never be perfect. Instead of depressing me, this knowledge causes me to *want* to grow. I no longer feel like running away from myself, and that makes me smile. I'm committed to living the remainder of my days lovingly and peacefully with the person inside me.

One day I wrote in my journal, "Good morning, Joan. Let's be Forever Friends."

Lord, thank You that I no longer live in enmity
with myself or with You.

Make It Personal: How about making a list of the kind things you do to show your friends you love them? Then choose one of those things to do for yourself. Put this "love gift" on your schedule so that you won't forget, and take time to write a short friendship note to give yourself with the gift. (Send me an email after you do this to let me know how it goes!)

Silence: Not Always Golden

Then Jesus and his followers left that place and went through
Galilee. He didn't want anyone to know where he was, because he
was teaching his followers. He said to them, "The Son of Man will
be handed over to people, and they will kill him. After three days,
he will rise from the dead." But the followers did not understand
what Jesus meant, and they were afraid to ask him.

Mark 9:30-32

This story in Mark fascinates me. Jesus, the best Teacher ever, made intentional travel plans so that He could communicate specifically with His team. He shared about the approaching death and reappearance of the Son of Man. It wasn't the first time Jesus referred to Himself as the Son of Man (see Mark 2:10,28; 8:31,38; 9:9).

Jesus' message understandably confused His followers. He looked healthy and safe to them at the moment. Yet though they didn't *get* it, they neglected to ask questions. They were too afraid.

I think we're sometimes like those frightened disciples. Instead of admitting our confusion, fear or misunderstanding, we clam up, change the subject and talk to others instead of asking for clarity from the source of the confusion (it appears that Jesus' team did all three; see Mark 9:33-34).

Like the woman whose daughter continues to lose weight but who refuses to ask her about it, sometimes our fear (or discomfort) causes us to retreat and remain silent. But silence isn't always golden. We *can* learn to challenge our fear, admit our uncertainty, ask for clarification and then face the future together.

Lord, help me speak up when
I don't understand.

Make It Personal: This week, consider breaking your silence to ask about something that confuses you.

Giving Grief Dignity

My eyes will flow unceasingly, without relief,
until the LORD looks down from heaven and sees.

Lamentations 3:49

"It's been over a year now; still I feel like my heart's torn in two," said my widow friend. "Some tell me to get on with life. Others think I should never enjoy myself again. I don't know. I'm doing the best I can. I suppose I *should* do better, but I just feel so alone." This woman grieves in solitude or buries her feelings partly because she doesn't want to bother others with her pain and the way she deals with it.

Mourning tragic loss is messy and difficult. We may doubt our sanity and God's compassion. The author of the book of Lamentations wrote heart-wrenching poems expressing his sorrow. God didn't say, "Your book is too depressing to be included in the Bible." Eugene Peterson, the well-respected pastor and Bible scholar, writes, "Lamentations keeps company with the extensive biblical witness that gives dignity to suffering by insisting that God enters our suffering and is companion to our suffering."[30]

God allows us the time we need to heal. He doesn't require that we hurry and get on with it or that we keep crying forever in order to show our love and loyalty. There's no perfect way to grieve. What breaks your heart breaks God's heart, too.

Lord, I'm tired of trying to grieve
perfectly. Please help me.

Make It Personal: What resources do you need to help you in your grief and loss? If you don't know, consider asking a caring and knowledgeable expert (a doctor, counselor or other professional) to share with you in your pain.

Inputting Misinformation

Surely you desire truth
in the inner parts.

Psalm 51:6

"We followed the directions and it still doesn't work," I said. "I'm tired."

"Me, too. I'm taking a break," responded my husband. We had worked all day installing a new financial program onto our computer. Several hours earlier, when we thought we were finished, we discovered a large discrepancy in our checking account reconciliation. We read the manual repeatedly and implemented the instructions, but nothing changed. We were stumped and exhausted.

I scanned the screen for the umpteenth time. Then I saw it! "Richard, come here," I shouted. Our problem? We had informed the computer we owned $5,000 more than we did. When we told the computer the truth, the checkbook balanced and the software worked.

For years, I fed my mental computer misinformation about life, others, God and myself. I didn't realize that's what I was doing. After all, I followed Jesus, prayed and studied my Bible. Yet after constantly inputting half-truths, I emerged in mid-life perplexed and worn out, trying to understand why my life didn't work the way I wanted it to work.

Although it felt unfamiliar and uncomfortable, I decided to identify my confusing lies and start telling myself the truth.[31] As I did, I found courage to change the unhelpful behavior that resulted from believing those lies. The change didn't happen as instantly as with my computer, but it started a transformative process within me.

Lord, help me figure out my misconceptions
and replace them with the truth.

Make It Personal: What are you telling yourself right now? Does that work for you or against you? In what way?

Adjusting Childhood Impressions

So in everything, do to others what you would have them do to you.
Matthew 7:12

As a child, the Golden Rule intrigued me. I asked myself, *What do I want others to do to me?* After some thought, I determined that I wanted others to be nice to me, to listen, to support my ideas, to approve of me, and to compliment and love me.

Consequently, I decided to do *to* and *for* others what I wanted for myself. I thought that if I did to others what I imagined they wanted, they would reciprocate. It worked! People frequently treated me well. I found the secret to satisfying relationships . . . or so I thought.

As an adult, however, my concept was incomplete. Because I had to always "be nice," I couldn't be honest about my feelings and perceptions. Sometimes others took advantage.

The strengths you and I gain in childhood help us become productive adults. But strength pushed to excess functions as weakness. For example, my ability to listen is a favorable attribute. But if I neglect to share who I am, then listening only hinders me from developing mutually rewarding relationships.

I've adjusted my childhood understanding of the Golden Rule with the following: "Do for and to others with the same respect, dignity and honesty you wish shown to and for you."

Lord, help me to treat others in an
equal and caring manner.

Make It Personal: List two of your strengths and two of your weaknesses. What do you notice about your list? What did you learn in childhood that isn't working well for you as an adult? How will you redefine that childhood concept?

God Is on Your Side

*Do you not know that your body is a temple of the
Holy Spirit, who is in you, whom you have received from God? . . .
Therefore honor God with your body.*

1 Corinthians 6:19-20

Today I talked with two lovely Christian women about body dissatisfaction. "I want to lose weight," Lori[32] said, "but I keep sabotaging myself. I'm tired of stressing about it. I always believed my body was merely the container for my brain and soul, yet after learning 1 Corinthians 6:19-20, I understand that my body itself is important to God. I'm going to stop shaming myself and look for good ways to treat my body."

Jeanne[33] said, "When I'm frustrated with aging or my lack of physical attractiveness, I remember how God has gifted me with functional beauty. For example, I feel healthy when exercising and running a marathon. Four babies received life and nourishment from my body. I love and support my husband. My hands prepare meals; my smile and listening ear comfort hurting friends. These flow from the inner beauty I truly desire" (see 1 Peter 3:4).

Each woman approaches this topic from a slightly different paradigm, yet both agree: I'm God's creation, housed in the only body I'll ever have. He cares about every part of me, and I'll join Him in honoring and taking care of my body.

*Lord, I don't understand exactly why I'm made
like I am. Yet I know that You're on my side and You want
me to enjoy the body You have given me.*

Make It Personal: Name several ways God shows you that He's on your side. Now list two ways you will honor God with your unique body.

Setting Myself Free

*Is this not the kind of fasting I have chosen . . .
to set the oppressed free? . . . Then your light will break
forth like the dawn, and your healing will quickly appear . . .
and the glory of the Lord will be your rear guard.*

Isaiah 58:6,8

"Joan, what keeps you from making your needs and desires known?" asks my long-time friend.

"I don't want to do it wrong," I invariably reply. I usually plan long and hard before asking for what I need, because I want to make any requests correctly. Don't the how-to books stress how important that is? Genuinely wanting my interactions to be above reproach, I try harder— and often end up confusing others by not expressing my thoughts and desires. Instead of liberating me as I think it will, this approach tightens the band around my chest, restricts my breathing and allows others to take advantage.

Here's what I've learned: No matter how hard I work, care and serve, my life in this imperfect world (and the way I relate to my life) can never be flawless. I'm human and limited. I won't always know how to express myself. As I accept this reality, I'm then free to enjoy God's presence and receive His insight, healing and protection.

*Lord, I need help. I want to break the chains
of rigidity and set myself free.*

Make It Personal: Read today's verse again. Ask God for healing and insight (light breaking forth like the dawn!) and protection (the Lord's glory will be your rear guard!).

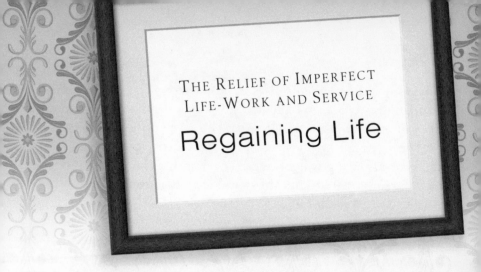

Regaining Life

"I'm working as hard as I can, yet accomplishing less," wrote a conscientious and caring Christian woman in her journal. "It's confusing. I used to enjoy being with others, but lately people irritate me. (Doesn't matter what age—8 or 88!) It's hard to get up in the morning. And right now I don't much like who I am. Sometimes I want to go away and hide. I'm praying, but it doesn't seem to do any good. Who cares anyway?"

These words reveal classic over-working and over-serving symptoms gone haywire. Unless steps are taken to halt the downward spiral, this capable woman could become another charred statistic. There are no simple solutions to this dilemma, yet a key step in becoming mentally and emotionally strong again is to accept responsibility for one's self. Accepting responsibility means making decisions to reverse sabotaging thoughts and over-loaded behavior. Yet someone facing possible burnout cringes at the mere thought of *doing* something. Doing is what drove her into this suffocating corner. However, this time the *doing* is not in the name of accomplishment, success or service. This doing is to *regain life*. I know. I remember. This woman was me.

When I share my story, some nod. Others laugh. "Not me," they say. Yet my experience (life-coaching, life-planning, speaking, mentoring in places around the world) is that more women than admit it struggle with issues related to work and service. It's epidemic, and it matters not if the woman is an executive, nurse, homeschooler, ministry volunteer or young wife and mother. In her book *Working Ourselves to Death*, Diane Fassel maintains that though workaholics may work a great deal, they aren't *always* working. The "work anorexic," afraid she'll make a mistake, procrastinates and then feels so guilty that she's immobilized. The "work binger" works in high-intensity spurts that become her method of medicating life's disappointments. The most noticeable workaholic is the "obsessive worker," who accepts project after project, working long hours to ensure it gets done right. (I'm chuckling. Its 9:30 P.M. I've been working since 7:00 A.M. and I'm off to bed without feeling guilty or overwhelmed. No wonder I smile.)

It's what we *believe* about work and service that pushes us into the burnout furnace. We adopt half-truths as our daily mantras: *God calls me to work for Him and never let up. I must give myself away tirelessly. I should be a flawless witness. I must accomplish for God. He expects perfection, total righteousness, from me. I can't disappoint Him or others. God doesn't fail. I'm His representative. I can't fail.*

Yet God knows the truth: He is perfect, tireless and almighty; we are not. He lovingly gifts and empowers us, yet merely because we're asked to and we *can* meet a need or fill the position doesn't mean that we *must*. God allows finite human beings (that's you and me!) to live within the confines of time and space to protect us from work overload and burnout—and to help us live in harmony with our humanness.

A wise friend says, "*No* is a complete sentence." *Indeed.* Even Jesus—who came to this imperfect earth to show us God and become our Savior—said no sometimes (see Luke 8:26-38; Mark 5:18-20).

God *wants* us to loosen the grip we have on our life-work and service. Enjoyment, relaxation, renewal and play are precious tokens of His loving generosity. He is not a slave driver. If you're one of the 60 million American women who Dr. Brent W. Bost claims are so overscheduled and overstressed that it affects your physical health, God invites you to slow down, relax and adjust your unrealistic expectations.[34] You will still be a valuable, caring and productive woman. Your work and service don't have to be relentless or perfect to be wonderful and significant. *Now that's a smile-able truth!*

Reversing Direction

I denied myself nothing my eyes desired . . . my heart took
delight in all my work . . . Yet when I surveyed all that my hands
had done and what I had toiled to achieve, everything was
meaningless, a chasing after the wind.

Ecclesiastes 2:10-11

"I want to be a rich workaholic. I just want to be rich and work all the time and enjoy my job," wrote a high school senior in an article I read. This teenager's words rang warning sirens for me. *If she only knew what she's really wishing for herself,* I thought.

Another definition for workaholism is *addiction to action.* (We may have a pandemic of actionaholism today!) Experts agree that workaholics (actionaholics) suffer from irrational fixations with work and doing. Symptoms may include compulsive rushing and busyness, constant thinking about work or performance, continual list-making, reluctance or inability to relax, diminished family and social life, and neglect of self-care. Workaholism is a progressive disease. Left unattended, it can kill us. (Doctors are treating increasing numbers of women who exhibit various disorders related to what the medical community calls the "hurried syndrome."[35])

Yet we have a choice. We can reverse our direction. Although not easy, we can cease chasing after the wind. God is on our side. Life can and will have new meaning.

*Lord, release me from my action
addiction tendencies so that at the end of my life
I can look back and smile.*

Make It Personal: Which of the above-listed symptoms do you exhibit? On a scale of 0 ("Not a problem for me") to 10 ("Headed off the charts"), where are you now?

Unlikely Blessings

*Is your life full of difficulties and temptations? Then be
happy, for when the way is rough, your patience has a chance
to grow. So let it grow . . . For when your patience is finally
in full bloom, . . . you will be . . . strong in character.*

James 1:2-4, *TLB*

I'm sitting alone looking out the window of the log cabin where I'm retreating this week (a delight this recovering action addict once thought impossible). I'm surrounded by stately pine trees waving gently at me under the intensely blue Arizona sky.

This setting reminds me of something I once read: Jack pine and lodgepole pine trees produce seed-filled pine cones that may cling to an overloaded tree for 20 years. Yet germination never occurs until the intense heat of a forest fire causes the cones to shed, dropping seeds to the fertile cooled ashes below. Only after the fire can new growth take place.

I wondered if anything remotely useful could result from my burned-out years. Yet out of the white heat of that burnout, I grew—and God has asked me to share what I've learned with others.

Burnout allowed me the opportunity to reevaluate my priorities, ask God for help, adjust my actions and develop greater effectiveness. It took awhile for me to appreciate the benefits, but I'm seeing the blessings now. Although God didn't cause my burnout, He and I are partnering to use it for good.

*Lord, help me believe that I can
be blessed through these difficulties.*

Make It Personal: What unpleasantness has God used in your life for good?

Entrance to Freedom

Not to us, but to your name be the glory,
because of your love and faithfulness.

Psalm 115:1

A friend said to me after weeks of 10- to 12-hour work days, "Joan, please pray I won't become resentful of all the things I must do. Seems like the demands are grabbing all at once."

"Certainly I'll pray for you," I responded. "What demands are pressing at you?"

"Oh, you know. My job, the overtime, my children and husband, my ailing parents, the Sunday School class I teach, my Bible study group, the softball team I coach—for starters."

"You feeling burned out, Nicole?" I asked.

"Maybe," she replied.

Gradually, my friend learned that her thinking included the philosophy that author Carmen Renee Berry calls the "Messiah Trap." The trap includes two fallacies: "If I don't do it, it won't get done" and "Everyone else's needs take priority over mine." Believing these lies landed Nicole on the highway to exhaustion. It's not a road she wished to take; it's one that overtook her—and she felt trapped, no exit in sight.

Nicole tried to do more than humanly possible. She *taught* others to take advantage of her willingness and then her God-given self-care boundaries got trampled.[36] That's when resentment loomed. Yet awareness of this predicament triggered her healing and the transfer of glory back to the God she served. God lovingly and faithfully lifted Nicole from the trap and set her on the road to recovery and relief.

O Lord, sometimes I feel trapped.
Please help me find the entrance to freedom.

Make It Personal: What would free you up? What one step will you take in that direction?

The Getaway

*Oh, that I had the wings of a dove! I would fly away
and be at rest . . . far from the . . . storm.*

Psalm 55:6,8

"All people in burnout develop the feeling that they want to just run away and hide from the world. Part of the reason for this is that they *do* need to get away from the source of the problem," says Myron D. Rush, author of *Burnout.*[37] Specialists in the burnout field insist that the first step toward healing is to move away from the fire. This proves difficult for most. It was for me.

Struggling about whether or not to leave the company I helped to start, I kept repeating, "I can't leave my baby!"[38]

My husband listened and finally responded, "Please stop calling it your baby. Your children are in the next room." His words shocked me back to reality.

I *did* leave, hoping to heal. Yet I continued to work freelance, and six months later I still wanted to run away. My family and I agreed that going away to recuperate was wise. So, struggling for equilibrium, I traveled across the country to be alone. Frequently during that time, I contemplated never returning. But I did come back to face my reality and heal.

Each woman's situation—and getaway solution—is unique. Yet this truth remains: Wherever she goes, God never leaves her. *I love that!*

*Lord, please see me safely
through this season.*

Make It Personal: Even though you don't feel burned-out, consider planning a simple getaway. A few hours at the park? Evening out? Overnighter? What resources do you need for this to happen? When will you do it?

Touching Tranquility

Better one handful with tranquility than two handfuls
with toil and chasing after the wind.

Ecclesiastes 4:6

For years, I had the overwhelming feeling that I must keep both hands full with assignments, jobs and clients. If a project threatened to fall between my fingers, I panicked.

One day, a coworker and I were so busy trying to meet deadlines that it was almost comical. But I wasn't laughing. "Do you ever worry you won't get it all done and everyone will be angry and go elsewhere?" I asked.

She eyed me strangely and answered, "No."

Is something wrong with me? I wondered, and then continued racing through my day. I felt compelled to prove I was worthy to be alive. I wanted desperately to please my husband and make him proud. I was chasing after the wind.

Although it's an ongoing and imperfect journey, I've learned that I don't need both hands full with work and service. Several months ago, as I talked to God about the pressure I felt and asked Him what I should do about all the goals, deadlines and needs before me, He seemed to affirm something He'd shown me before: "Do what you can, Joan, and I'll do the rest." I relaxed. Then I wondered if I'd heard Him correctly. Apparently I did, since He has repeated this message numerous times since then.

I don't have to chase to guarantee it all. *Whew.* Life feels more balanced with one hand toiling and the other touching tranquility.

Lord, thank You for the reminder that it's possible
to balance work with sane daily living.

Make It Personal: What would bring you tranquility today?

Adrenaline Junkie

Heal me, O Lord, and I will be healed . . .
for you are the one I praise.

Jeremiah 17:14

"You really love this, don't you, Joan?" said my customer. "You come alive when you're working." This comment came from the first client I took after my burnout necessitated a sabbatical. As she spoke, I felt my stomach tighten. I had tried so hard to leave my trying-too-hard-to-make-it-all-just-right lifestyle. (Ironic, huh?)

I do get a certain high when rushing, working and finding solutions. I am an "adrenaline junkie." Experts say the "busy" disease (probably related to the "hurried syndrome" I've already mentioned) is both a process and a substance addiction. The substance is the chemical adrenaline. As long as the chemical flows, we medicate the pain and disappointments of life. I guess that's what I did for years and, like other addictions, it seemed to soothe my discontent and take my mind off the problems I refused to confront.

However, when the chemical turned on me and started messing with my physical, emotional and mental wellbeing, I asked the Master Healer for help. I accept that it's a messy process for me sometimes. Yet I'm learning to better manage life's inevitable disappointments and cultivate a healthy association with my work. Along with Jeremiah, I praise God for His healing touch.

Lord God, I believe Your healing intervention
can restore my sense of wellbeing. I promise
to cooperate with Your treatment.

Make It Personal: When, where and with whom do you tend to over-hurry? How can this awareness benefit you right now?

Have Fun!

He makes me lie down in green pastures,
he leads me beside quiet waters,
he restores my soul.

Psalm 23:2-3

After living in our house for 14 years, I finally walked up the hill that overlooked our housing development. For the first time, I gazed above the treetops and noticed the new steeple on the oldest church in our community. To the south, I saw the high school that our children attended. I recalled the long-ago days when my son and daughter slid down the hill on their snow sleds. Although I knew where they were and what they were doing, I never came along.

In one sense, I didn't have time to explore that day. I'm glad I did, however, because after 20 minutes I returned to my work with a renewed attitude.

I'm not a machine, cranking out productivity. I am a living, breathing part of God's creation. He gives me each new day as His current masterpiece to enjoy.

*Lord, I have so much to do. Still I'm
going to take a break. Breathe fresh air
into my mind and soul.*

Make It Personal: Are you overwhelmed and pressured by a heavy work or family load? Do unfinished projects, obligations and deadlines threaten your contentment? I suggest you take a mini-vacation. Walk by a quiet stream, sit in the grass, climb a hill. Do that fun activity that you've been longing to do—or something you've never done before. Think of it as a soul-restoring gift from your loving Creator.

What did you decide to do? When? If it will help you keep that appointment with yourself, write it on your calendar. Go ahead; have fun!

70

Sounds Sensible to Me

In vain you rise early and stay up late, toiling.

Psalm 127:1-2

The deadline for an important project rushes toward me.

Similar jobs have taken longer than the time I have. How can I do it? Say no to something else, because I've said yes to this project? Done that. Skip meals? Passing up nutrition no longer works for me. What's left? Work harder and longer. But previous experience indicates I can no longer deny my human time/energy limitations. I've got to sleep. Now what?

"Contrary to Conventional Wisdom . . . the next time you are faced with a difficult task, remember a passionate 90 percent is better than a panicked 110 percent," writes author Robert Kreigel.[39] Sounds sensible to me. So, first I'll ask for a deadline extension and if that's not possible, I'll alleviate some of my time-panic by:

- Limiting the number of hours I spend on each specific phase
- Refusing ineffective over-analyzing and worry
- Asking for assistance
- Being satisfied with the best I can do at the moment and not expecting perfection

You and I aren't superwomen. We can't stuff additional accomplishments into a limited time span merely by *willing* to do so. Going faster and trying harder often crush creativity and decrease productivity. When I work in cooperation with my limitations, I experience less stress. How about you?

Lord, help me to be reasonable about my expectations.
And to realize that less is sometimes more.

Make It Personal: Which of the above suggestions will you practice this week?

Mark of a Perfect Perfectionist

To all perfection I see a limit.

Psalm 119:96

For months, I meticulously planned for a statewide writing seminar. I wrote confirmation letters, signed contracts, made phones calls and took notes. Schedules and menus were verified, deposits made and attendance counts submitted.

I arrived at the hall on the designated morning to discover the speaker and board members standing on the sidewalk in the cold. All doors were locked. A security guard drove by, felt sorry for us and let us in. Once inside, we found no podium, microphone or breakfast setup. I made some phone calls and half an hour later learned that the mix-up was due to someone's faulty alarm clock. He would take a shower, get dressed and come set up for us. Obviously, this would happen past our starting time.

We had no control over these circumstances, but we had a choice: We could ignore reality (remember, that's the mark of a perfect perfectionist!) and force through our perfectly planned agenda, consequently experiencing mounting stress, or we could smile, be flexible and bypass the frustration.

We chose to laugh and start the seminar late. The situation confirmed to me again that trying to be a perfect person in an imperfect world is impossible. It also showed me something else: *I can change.* And that's no small miracle! Thank You, Lord.

Lord, there are obvious limits to all my perfect planning.
Help me learn to be flexible and adjust to changing circumstances.

Make It Personal: What happened to you this week that you had absolutely no control over? What did you like or not like about how you handled it?

More Than Your Share

Buy the truth . . . do not sell it.

Proverbs 23:23

"I accepted a job caring for 7 to 9 children each morning, and 15 to 20 kids showed up," my friend told me. "Although frustrating and exhausting, I tolerated it for weeks. When I casually mentioned the overcrowded conditions to my manager, he seemed unconcerned. I coped as long as I could and then resigned. On my last day, I overheard the boss tell my replacement, 'You'll never have more than 7 to 9 children.' I couldn't believe he would fib so deliberately!

"Later, I learned that within 5 days, the new employee insisted on additional help. My former boss said he wasn't aware there were so many children in the daycare room and immediately hired assistance. Can you believe that?" exclaimed my friend.

Sometimes our over-working and silence contribute to misunderstandings about the truth. Once we comprehend this, perhaps we can give ourselves permission to change. In their bestselling book *Boundaries*, Dr. Henry Cloud and Dr. John Townsend write, "Remember that your job overload is your responsibility and your problem. If your job is driving you crazy, you need to do something about it. . . . Stop being a victim . . . and start setting some limits."[40] This advice holds true for executives, homeschoolers, church staff and volunteers. It's okay with God to speak up. He's pleased when we buy the truth and never forfeit it.

Lord, my "I must endure it all" thinking
is exhausting to me and confusing to others.
Give me courage to set boundaries.

Make It Personal: In what area are you doing more than your share of the work? Consider sharing this reality with the appropriate persons.

Ditching Man-made Rules

"Come to me, all you who are weary and burdened . . .
Take my yoke upon you and learn from me, for I am gentle
and humble in heart, and you will find rest for your souls.
For my yoke is easy and my burden is light."

Matthew 11:28-30

"I really want to follow Christ," my friend said, "but I'm tired of trying so hard to do it right. How could Jesus say His way is easy?"

I understood what she meant. Many confusing *shoulds, oughts* and *have-tos* had been impressed into my spiritual thinking as well. You *should* forget yourself. You *must* never complain. You *ought to* give until it hurts. *Never* get angry. *Always* take care of yourself. You *must* be nice all the time. *Never* skip church. You *should always* be ready to serve. *Never* listen to your feelings. You *must* read your Bible every day. *Always* discern. *Never* judge.

When human ultimatums are added to God's loving directives, the Christian life becomes burdensome. This is not what Jesus wants for me—or for you.

Jesus says, "The yoke—work, job, life, ministry—I have for you is unique. It fits you. Learn from Me. We'll do it together. Live for Me, not for the approval of those who make the burdensome rules. I offer respite when you're tired, not more regulations. I promise."

Lord, I'm going to ditch the man-made
rules and accept what You have for me.
Teach me. I need some rest.

Make It Personal: Think of a time you sensed Jesus' "yoke" fit you. What was happening?

The Horse Race

In quietness and trust is your strength, but you would
have none of it. You said, "No, we will flee on horses."

Isaiah 30:15-16

"Stop striving to be just like your wayward neighbors," God said to the Israelite people. "You don't necessarily need more horses, armies and weapons. Cease running around. Be quiet; trust Me. I have a plan." But they didn't listen. They were more comfortable with their own strategies. Racing horses made more sense to them.

Keith Miller, in his book *Hope in the Fast Lane*, writes, "I don't know whether or not you . . . can know what it is like to be a driven person . . . [to go] to bed, staring at the ceiling, feeling frantic about the fact that you have more to do the next day than you can possibly get done. . . . This compulsive working/committing has been a way of life for me. . . . So for me to be living a quiet, sane life, . . . instead of at a high-pressure, high-anxiety pace, is indeed like being born again."[41]

Like the Israelites and Keith Miller, I've sometimes been more familiar with racing horses than with being quiet, breathing deeply and trusting God. My spirituality isn't proved by merely rushing to accomplish and provide solutions. I'm loved and valued by God when being quiet and still, as well.

*Thank You, Lord, for offering me
rest from the "horse race."*

Make It Personal: What did God *show* you the last time you were quiet together? As He had for the Israelites, He has a plan for you. How about setting aside some time to listen for what He's saying to you now?

About Sleeping . . .

Do not let yourselves be burdened again by a yoke of slavery.

Galatians 5:1

"I'm tired. When my husband's gone, I don't sleep much."

"You said he travels with his job every week. You must be tired *a lot!*" I concluded.

"I guess I am," my new friend admitted. We had met at a seminar. "This morning I paused to ask myself, *What's up with this?*"

"Your answer?" I asked.

"If I go to sleep, I'll be wasting time. I should make good use of each minute."

This competent woman's inner slave driver insists, *Your value depends on how well you spend each second. Stay busy. Don't waste any precious moments. Keep an account of every hour.*

Mark Buchanan, author of *The Rest of God*, writes, "The refusal of rest amounts to: living as though the taskmasters still hover and glower ever ready to thrash us for the smallest sign of slowing down."[42] Perhaps, like my new friend, you've submitted to the taskmaster in your head and it's wearing you out. She replaced her slave driver's message with a more respectful—and true—one: *I'm valuable even when I'm not busy. I can go to sleep at a sensible hour and still be a productive person.*

"Sleep, besides being a necessity, is also an act of faith," Buchanan maintains. "We give ourselves, regardless of our unfinished business, into God's care. We sleep simply because we believe God will look after us."[43] That's great news to me.

Lord, thanks for loving and accepting me
whether I'm working or sleeping.

Make It Personal: Consider going to sleep 15 minutes earlier several nights this week.

Mr. Should Bully

*Whatever I have, wherever I am, I can make it through
anything in the One who makes me who I am.*

Philippians 4:12-13, *THE MESSAGE*

"What's up?" asks my coach.

"I feel scattered, unfocused," I reply. "All these to-dos glare at me. Proposals and websites to create. Clients and emails to answer. Marketing/publicity tasks to complete."

"Your unfinished tasks are taking up a lot of space, aren't they?"

"Yes, but something tells me I shouldn't have unfinished tasks; I should be done."

"Sounds like an inner bully. How about getting him out of your head to talk?"

"You think you're helping, but you're not," I say to the imaginary bully. To my coach, I declare, "Now I feel even more agitated."

"Pretend you're on the playground during recess. The unfinished-tasks bully is harassing you and the teacher's not standing up for you."

"I feel like the bully has a right to harass me, but I feel bruised." *Aha!* "I guess I believe in order to get my work done, I need to bully myself."

"What are you going to do about it?" asks my coach.

"Sit down and shut up, Bully," I say to my inner taskmaster. "I can do it without you egging me on." I feel relieved. And I feel stupid because the remedy is so simple. Then I laugh and admit, "*Should* happens!"

I don't need to brow beat myself into achievement—or heed my inner bully. I can do all that God asks me to do through Christ's strength. I'll listen to Him.

*Lord, please help me silence
my Mr. Should Bully.*

Make It Personal: What will you tell your inner bully?

Wide-open Space

I will be glad and rejoice in your love, for you saw . . . the anguish
of my soul. You have . . . set my feet in a spacious place.

Psalm 31:7-8

I did what I assumed I should and allowed a few inner and outer bullies to dictate how I ought to be: *You're selfish. Try harder. Get it all done.*
He's mad at you. You should do more. You gotta look better. You don't need rest.
I felt confined to a narrow box with little space for developing creativity, intimacy or individuality—all the things I longed for.

After years of living this way, I felt deep anguish. But if I kept busy
enough, I didn't have to deal with the disappointment or hurt. Then it
backfired and I crashed. "Help, Lord," I cried. "I can't do it anymore."
And He met me in my mess. About that time, I read Psalm 31:7-8 and
my exhausted heart smiled. *I don't have to stay in the box!*

Even now, every time I read His promise to set my feet in a spacious
place, I smile—inside and out. I want to tell any woman (or man) who
feels trapped that God will open the lid of your box and take you to a
wide-open space. He wants to release you from the limitations of your
misconceptions and set you in a place of expanded joy.

Lord, You see me here. I want out.
Please lead to a freer place.

Make It Personal: What's your spacious place look like to you? Ask
God to take you there.

Sitting with Jesus

"Martha . . ." the Lord answered, "You are worried and upset about
many things, but one thing is needed. Mary has chosen what
is better, and it will not be taken away from her."

Luke 10:41-42

Martha, the original actionaholic, was genuinely concerned with serving others, but her service—helping, caring, doing—controlled her. Although she planned and prepared delicious meals, her guests may have felt she cared more about her good deeds than about them. Martha lived centuries ago, yet her trying-too-hard-to-make-it-all-just-right lifestyle remains prevalent today.

Like Martha, we get dragged around by our action addiction, misconceptions and over-doing. "Busyness, by itself, breeds distraction. . . . Martha opened her home to Jesus, but that doesn't automatically mean she opened her heart. In her eagerness to serve Jesus, she almost missed the opportunity to *know* Jesus," explains Joanna Weaver in her book *Having a Mary Heart in a Martha World*.[44]

When we cut the leash on our habitual doing, working and people pleasing, we can relax a little and, like Mary, learn to sit with Jesus. It is at Jesus' feet that you and I understand who we are and how we can become the persons God created us to be. In His presence, we find help for dealing with life's disappointments and experience God's unconditional love and acceptance.

*Lord, I get so tired. Sometimes life seems to
control me, instead of me controlling it. Please help me
to balance my doing with quiet listening.*

Make It Personal: Remember a time you enjoyed sitting with Jesus. What was it like? When will you sit with Him again?

Can Bitter Be Sweet?

They say that what is right is wrong, and what is wrong is right;
that black is white and white is black, bitter is sweet and sweet is bitter.

Isaiah 5:20, *TLB*

"You certainly have mega responsibility," I said. "How are you doing in your job at church?"

"I'm handling the pressure well," she responded. "Unlike in my corporate VP job, where I completely burned out, I'm getting everything done here and all is sweet."

I wanted to believe her, yet evidence pointed to an opposite reality. Those she worked with admitted they felt confused because she had little time to explain procedures. Deadlines were missed, Bible study dates and curriculum often changed, follow-up was neglected, and the laypeople under her care regularly dropped out. She had agreed to a part-time position (30 hours per week), but for months she had worked 50 or more each week. Senior church staff sent mixed signals and, instead of addressing the issue, she kept trying to make it work.

It wasn't working.

My friend, like those written about in the book of Isaiah, insisted that black was white and sour was sweet. Expert at convincing herself that all was well, loved ones watched and wondered how this intelligent woman could be so confused.

When we pretend our obsessive work/service behavior is healthy, we hurt ourselves and others, even though we don't want to. Life makes more sense when we admit that black can't appear white, bitter won't taste sweet, and pretending doesn't mix with fruitful leadership. Admitting the unpleasant truth allows the good to emerge. We *can* change.

Lord, please give me clarity.

Make It Personal: What are you pretending to know—or not know? When do you maintain everything is "sweet" and yet it tastes "bitter"?

Setting Mini-goals

Therefore do not worry about tomorrow,
for tomorrow will worry about itself.

Matthew 6:34

Sometimes when I set a long-range goal, I find it tricky to relax until it's completed. This means an extended project can propel me into perpetual angst (evidenced by the knots on both sides of my neck). According to the "Excellence vs. Perfectionism" chart in my book *The Relief of Imperfection*, this characteristic is a bona fide symptom of perfectionism. When caught in the pursuit for perfection, my focus is on the finished product and I miss the daily fun. But by practicing excellence, my focus is on the process with its surprising learning opportunities. I *get* this, but I still want *how-to* help.

Dr. David Stoop, author of *Living with a Perfectionist*, suggests setting sub-goals in the quest to finish a larger objective. I first tried this method after I signed a contract to write 365 stories for a children's devotional book. Although a huge project (my first publishing attempt), I broke it down into mini-goals of completing four stories per day. When I started feeling overwhelmed with the enormity of the total job, I reminded myself that since I had finished the daily quota, I could chill out. I was free to enjoy myself and others without preoccupation with unfinished business.

God doesn't expect us to complete our entire life's to-do list in one week! Jesus assured us of this when He said, "Don't focus on tomorrow. Be satisfied with your *today*."

Lord, help me to be pleased
with daily progress.

Make It Personal: Which large project or task will you break into mini-goals? How?

Work 'til You Drop

We hope that your faith will grow and that, still within the limits
set for us, our work among you will be greatly enlarged.

2 Corinthians 10:15, *TLB*

"I'm exhausted. Worked every day for months. Haven't had a real vacation in years. But I'm of hardy stock—the kind that keeps going until you drop. No matter. Once I drop, it's all over anyway. Right?" said the head chef of a catering company that supplied the meals to the Catholic Retreat Center I visited for silence and solitude. I overheard him chatting with the nuns on the center's staff. *Ironic, huh?*

Do we need to keep working and pushing until we collapse of exhaustion and die? Is that God's plan? It's true—and reasonable—that we all get tired while fulfilling our daily obligations. But some of us completely wear out by working too hard and too much in our service-related businesses, careers or ministries. As it was for this talented chef, it may be difficult for us to acknowledge our limitations, step back and let others take over for a little while so that we can rest and rejuvenate.

While we're away recharging our worn-out batteries, the work will go on. It may even grow and prosper. And when we return, we'll be better equipped to resume our daily responsibilities. We might even enjoy our work more.

*Lord, the apostle Paul recognized that he
had limits. So do I. I know I need to retreat and rest.
While I'm away, please continue to do Your will
in my work and ministry.*

Make It Personal: How was your last "R and R" (that is, rest and *relaxation*)? When will you take another?

Rest Regardless

He restores my soul.

Psalm 23:3

"Whenever I say I need to rest or take a nap, I get dirty looks from my family," said a coaching client. "This pushes my button and keeps me moving. Lately I've realized I let their reactions *control* me. Should I stop to rest even if they don't like it?"

This reminded me of a conversation I had with an executive friend, who said, "God has specifically told me to take care of myself this year and stop doing for everybody else what they can do for themselves or what someone other than me can do to help. He assured me that He doesn't want me to work so hard that my health is negatively affected. I will obey Him and include space and rest into my life. But here's the rub: Others don't appreciate that I've changed my *modus operandi*. I'm getting flack."

I understand. Some of us have *taught* others that we are super-women—willing, skilled and available to make life easier for them. When this is the case, it is unlikely that they'll suggest we relax, or be pleased if we choose to take time off. But here's what my client and the executive—and I—have learned: We don't have to wait until someone else notices our exhaustion and suggests we take a break. God grants us permission to take responsibility for ourselves. He loves to replenish our souls, and we can cooperate with Him regardless of what others say or do.

Lord, I want a balanced life of
doing, trusting and resting.

Make It Personal: What short and simple response will you make when someone questions your decision to take a break?

Delegating the Workload

The work is too heavy for you; you cannot handle it alone.

Exodus 18:18

"Moses, you're doing a great job of managing these 2 million people. And I do believe that God is on your side. Still, are you telling me all these people stand around from dawn until late at night so that they can tell you their problems and you can judge how to solve them? That's too much. You're going to burn out at this pace," warned Jethro, Moses' father-in-law.

Some of us, like Moses, are overcommitted. But we can admit our limitations, seek advice about establishing a plan and learn to delegate the workload. There are limits to what we can accomplish on our own. One of the clues in Moses' situation was that the people were waiting all day to get an appointment with him. Although Moses was responsible and caring, his organization wasn't running efficiently.

When we are engrossed in our working, serving and helping, it may be difficult to step aside, assess our needs and develop alternative methods. But we can ask for advice. Another person may be able to see the situation more clearly and offer help.

Jethro suggested that Moses appoint capable men to share his duties. We can develop a wise plan, too. Delegating our workload is acceptable to God.

Lord, I can't do it all. I want to relinquish
being in control of every detail. Please help me
establish a workable plan.

Make It Personal: What will you do to make your workload more manageable? What resources will you need? When will you start? Who will you ask for help?

No Formula Solutions

"It's more than action addiction or trying too hard to make it all just right. It's beyond jam-packed schedules and ambitious agendas. It goes past the tendency to say yes more often than no. While these contribute to our overloaded dilemma, something else is going on," I said to a diverse group of women gathered in a large banquet hall. "It includes media overload, financial overload, tech overload, sensory/Hollywood overload, info overload, overeating, over-shopping, over-dieting, over-studying, over-helping, over-knowing, over-achieving, over-choice and over-spiritualizing. It's *over-everything*!"

To my shock, a dignified-looking woman shouted, "Yes!" Soon, everyone at her table stood to cheer. They weren't applauding their maxed-out reality (or me, ha!), but that I had verbalized what they felt.

Our culture pushes the limits as far as possible and then pushes again. Even our churches seem to adopt the viewpoint that perfection (and boundlessness) is mandatory and attainable. It's like we honestly believe we can do bigger-better-more-faster and keep it up forever. Yet nothing on this earth is perfect! Not our ideas, service, talents, churches, pastors, programs, ministries or worship.

I'm grateful for the privilege of having served with many churches and Christian groups. Yet along with much good, I've received a few misguided messages. Here are two: (1) Christians should not express opposing (which is seen as negative) opinions, beliefs or emotions; (2) Christian leaders, whether at home or church, must appear right at all times. The problem is that when we believe message 2, message 1 must be enforced, because mistakes in judgment or internal flaws cannot be admitted. "The reality of all this is that you get *no* help for what's really going on in your life," write David Johnson and Jeff VanVonderen in *The Subtle Power of Spiritual Abuse*. "God's amazing grace has no chance to touch and heal it, because it is kept hidden."[45]

Sadly, I can recall tragic illustrations of this dangerous dynamic. In fact, I really don't want to think about the hurt and how it has touched those I love. As I write, I'm tempted to just get up from the computer and forget about it. I've seen the pain and what appears to be irrevocable damage done in the name of truth, power, right-ness, authority, God and spirituality—and it isn't fair. The truth is that spiritual leaders in churches, families and communities not only have human needs, limitations and imperfections (just like their followers), but some have unexamined emotional wounds and conditioned misbeliefs that compel them to treat others (and themselves) poorly, sometimes shamefully. I wish it were not so, but it is. Yet I sense God wants me to deliver a message of grace and relief in the midst of such imperfection. I'm humbled by how He has brought me to this point and what He is asking me to do, even though He is well aware that I'm an imperfect and completely human messenger!

So how do we find grace, gratitude and joy while experiencing the effects of both secular and Christian culture's heavy-going reality? I'm slim on the formula solutions here. What helps me right now is Jesus' gracious invitation to come to Him and rest. I don't believe God wants me to feel shamed, crushed or exhausted while navigating the Christian life *or* our bigger-better-more-faster culture. Jesus says to me—and you:

_____ [your name here], are you tired? Worn out? Burned out on religion? Come to me. Get away with me and you'll recover your life. I'll show you how to take a real rest. Walk with me and work with me—watch how I do it. Learn the unforced rhythms of grace. I won't lay anything heavy or ill-fitting on you. Keep company with me and you'll learn to live freely and lightly (Matthew 11:28-29, *THE MESSAGE*).

My final hope is knowing that one day I'll walk into Jesus' arms and be safe forever, even if I don't *get* it all now.

Holy Ground

To be absent from the body and
to be present with the Lord.

2 Corinthians 5:8, *NKJV*

My mother suffered repeated TIAs (transient ischemic attacks, or "mini strokes")[46] and lost her sight, hearing, reasoning and ability to talk. I hated what was happening to her. Then that dreaded call: "She's dying. Come." On Mother's fourth night at the hospital, my daughter, Lynnette, joined me.

"I wonder if Aunt Aileen will run to meet Grandma," said Lynnette. Mother and Aileen, who died the previous year, loved being sisters. While we chatted about heaven, mom's breathing turned more erratic. We watched her leave us. Kissing her cheek, I whispered, "This is Joanie, Mom. I love you. Tell Jesus hi for me." (For years, she had asked me to say hi to my friends each time I left the house.) Stroking her thinning white hair, I recalled how, as a child, I had combed her thick black locks. Lynnette wiped the lips that had often whispered, "Honey, you're special."

Death's messiness didn't terrify us as we imagined it would. Still, for weeks I tried to make sense of my emotions. Happy because life's disappointment and anger didn't matter to Mom anymore, I questioned the sad injustice of her disease and death *too soon*. One day God reassured me, "Joan, in that sterile hospital room, I sent angels to carry your mother to her Savior. You stood on holy ground" (see Acts 7:33).

Mom's debilitating disease, premature death and my own struggle with grief remind me of my flawed reality. Yet God's hope guarantees me life beyond the inequity and loss I feel.

*Lord, Your hope looms larger than
my pain and confusion. Thank You.*

Make It Personal: How has God placed hope in your heart?

Living Naturally

He gives strength to the weary and increases the power of the weak.
Even youths grow tired and weary and young men stumble and fall.

Isaiah 40:29-30

"Last year, I attempted to do more than a human being could reasonably do. It was unnatural and exhausting," said a charming and capable college junior. "So I've decided to reduce my unrealistic expectations for perfect grades this semester. I'm even going to say no to a few extracurricular activities. Just planning to be a natural young woman, not working so hard to hide my needs or dilemmas. I want to learn to laugh, feel, enjoy others and have some fun." I smiled when she shared her decision with me.

Learning to be natural (some might call it "genuinely normal") proves difficult in this bigger-better-more-faster culture in which we live and learn. Media, universities and even churches bombard us with "you're not enough, so do more" commercials, articles, competitions and pep talks. At the end of the day, week or year, we're just really tired.

Yet God offers us relief from the striving-too-hard-to-learn-and-do-more approach. He longs for us—whether young, middle-aged or older—to thrive as the women He designed us to be. Recording artist Amy Grant sings, "All I ever have to be is what you made me."[47] My lovely young "natural" friend is singing that song this year, too.

Lord, thank You that I don't have to be
any more or less than who You created me
to be. That's so energy renewing for me.

Make It Personal: What makes you laugh? Do a little of that this week.

Irrevocable Gifts

For God's gifts and his call are irrevocable.

Romans 11:29

"Perfectionists minimize their moral and ethical plus-side and magnify their failings," write Miriam Elliott and Susan Meltsner in the book *The Perfectionist Predicament*.[48] I've noticed this phenomenon in clients, friends, family members and, yes, even myself. (No surprise, huh?) I watched one woman hang her head in shame when her job circumstances prevented her from attending a church meeting. Another mentioned how bad she felt that her sick child kept her from having her private prayer time for a few days. The last few days, I've given myself grief for taking too long to write each devotion for this book. *What's wrong with you, Joan?* It's like we set up unrealistic spiritual expectations and then worry that God is disappointed in us.

However, here's what I'm learning (and I love it): God doesn't withdraw His grace, compassion or support when we fall short in our own eyes. Once we accept the invitation to be His child, He'll never change His mind. He gives us unique spiritual gifts and then employs us for service accordingly. God's gift of grace, as well as His promise to comfort, provide for and protect us, are undeserved benefits. His call and gifts are irrevocable.

Lord, I know that You've called me to love and
serve You. Everything You've given me is forever.
I'm filled with gratitude.

Make It Personal: How about putting a small gift box on your desk or dresser and then filling it with written reminders of God's irrevocable grace-filled gifts to you? Keep adding to your box during the next several months (or not—either way is okay).

Amazing Geese

Let us not give up meeting together . . .
let us encourage one another.

Hebrews 10:25

After moving from California to Minnesota, I couldn't help but notice the scores of geese that inhabit the beautiful lakes. During the first several months I lived there, I began to appreciate their unique habits.

In flight, each bird creates an uplift for the bird following behind. When flying in the familiar *V* formation, the entire flock experiences 71-percent increased flying range than if they flew alone.

As the lead bird gets tired, it flies back into the flock, and another bird takes over at the point position. It's not a big deal—they don't seem to fight over who gets to lead. Those in the rear ranks of the formation honk to encourage the front lines to keep up the speed needed to complete the journey.

Perhaps we can learn from the behavior patterns of the geese. Even though our churches, organizations, committees and families will never be perfectly supportive 24/7, it's to our advantage to accept and nurture the help and community of those who share our common goals and values. None of us can be the energizing leader all the time. Like these amazing geese, we can support one another in both the difficult and the fun tasks. After all, we're on this life journey together.

*Lord, sometimes I get so busy I neglect
my need for community. Help me remember to
look for the encouragement and support I need
and to allow others to do the same.*

Make It Personal: What kind of support would you like right now? Call and ask someone to "honk" for you.

Working Out

From him the whole body, joined and held together
by every supporting ligament, grows and builds itself
up in love, as each part does its work.

Ephesians 4:16

My son enjoys working out, and one time while spotting a friend lifting weights, he saw the man lose control. They heard a loud pop. Rich watched in shock as his friend's massive pectoral muscle detached and he writhed in pain. Not a pretty sight. This man pushed one part of his body too far.

Every Christian represents a unique part of Christ's Body, the collective Church. Arm muscles, shoulder muscles, leg muscles and ligaments all have particular functions. When each exercises his or her unique job, the entire Body is able to "work out" together. Yet when one person overextends, the Body is in danger of dysfunction.

I've noticed that some of us do our own tasks plus several other people's jobs as well. This creates unhealthy reliance on one part of the Body to the detriment of the whole. While a few succumb to burnout, others remain underdeveloped (speaking from personal experience, this isn't pretty).

Just as it's wise to treat all parts of our physical bodies with equal care, God proposes a good plan for exercising the whole Church Body. He intends for us to work together, supporting and building each other up in love—not necessarily because we're close friends, but because we care about one another's welfare. God's design helps us avoid individual burnout and promote healthy interdependence.

Lord, what is my part? I want to learn
to exercise it with compassion and balance.

Make It Personal: When have you experienced the benefit of God's good plan?

Unspoken Rules

We refuse to wear masks and play games. We don't
maneuver and manipulate behind the scenes. And we don't twist
God's Word to suit ourselves. Rather, we keep everything we do and
say out in the open, the whole truth on display, so that those who want
to can see and judge for themselves in the presence of God.

2 Corinthians 4:1-2, *THE MESSAGE*

When we strive too hard to be just right, we sometimes live by unspoken rules that have been passed down to us, which may include hidden by-laws like these:

- Don't talk about your own perceptions or feelings.
- Keep all problems or potential problems to yourself.
- Deny reality if it's less than perfect.
- Maintain the peace at any cost.
- Always agree, if you genuinely care about one another and desire unity.

Yet I've watched with respect as some have risked being labeled disloyal or unspiritual by refusing to play by the hidden rules. Recently, one courageous woman shared, "There's a silent assumption in our church that we'll all serve where the pastors say we should and read what they think we must. I'm weary of it." Like Paul, she's now committed to being upfront about what God is asking her to do, which creates freedom for others, as well. It's like grace and relief splashing all around her.

*Lord, I'm tired of playing by the hidden rules. I want to know
what You want for me. Please direct my decisions.*

Make It Personal: What do you sense God wants for you right now? Jot down your thoughts and ask Him for clarification. Come back to your notes in a week.

Adding Variety to Life

But each man has his own gift from God;
one has this gift, another has that.

1 Corinthians 7:7

At the college my daughter attended, the planning committee asked her to sing and me to accompany her on the piano at the Parent's Weekend final service. On the designated Sunday morning, hundreds of visiting parents, students and faculty filled the beautiful chapel. Glancing at the printed program, I noticed the special music included music majors and accomplished musicians. Doubts about our musical contribution pushed at the corners of my mind.

Prior to the service, all who were on the program met backstage to pray together. One student prayed, "Lord, thank You that although we each have different talents, it all fits together to make a complete program that honors You." Hearing those words, I relaxed.

While walking back to our seat my daughter asked, "Did you hear what the pianist prayed?"

"Yes, indeed," I replied.

She whispered back, "That's it! Even though I don't have the same type of voice as the senior music major, I can sing my song. And God will speak through both of us." She smiled and squeezed my hand.

We each have different gifts, talents and sounds. God planned it that way. When we do our individual part, the beautiful variation of God's creation shines through.

Lord, I look, sound and think differently than
my spiritual peers and leaders. That's okay.
It adds variety to life.

Make It Personal: What do you like doing that your sister, friend or mentor may not? Contemplate finding a way to enjoy living and serving in that uniqueness.

Focusing

For to me, to live is Christ.

Philippians 1:21

If the Internet existed in Paul's day, I think he would have communicated via email attachment. Not that it matters, but it's fun to think about his letter to the believers in Philippi flying through cyberspace. Even as a young Christian, I loved reading this joy-filled Bible book. Paul's words, "For to me, to live is Christ," fascinated me. *What did Paul mean? How does that impact me and other Christians?*

I began to recognize that Paul's main focus was not his ministry or work for Christ, but Christ Himself. I thought of Paul when I read this Oswald Chambers quote: "If I am devoted to the cause of humanity only, I will soon be exhausted and come to the place where my love will falter; but if I love Jesus Christ personally and passionately, I can serve humanity."[49]

When preoccupied with our ministry causes, we may try to accomplish the impossible through super-human strength. Then we'll be frustrated when others don't share our passion. Ministry devotion carried to an unhealthy extreme can lead to burnout.

Yet helping or ministering to others doesn't have to squeeze the joy out of life. Like Paul, we can turn our focus to the Source of all good deeds: Jesus Christ. In Him, we find freedom and energy to continue serving.

Lord, sometimes I wonder if I'm trying to prove that
I'm worthy to be Your child by allowing my ministry to
monopolize my time and thoughts. Really, You're my focus.
May that help to reduce my driven-ness.

Make It Personal: Type your response to this devotion in an email and send it to yourself.

How Paradoxical

They tie up heavy loads and put them on men's shoulders,
but they themselves are not willing to lift a finger to move them. . . .
For whoever humbles himself will be exalted.

Matthew 23:4,12

"I think I figured by persuading others to fit into my ideal image, I'd finally be satisfied with my life and work," said a ministry friend. "But it's not producing the results I want." (Yikes! Been there, done that!)

As in Jesus' day, sometimes ministry leaders tie up heavy loads of *shoulds* and *must-dos*, and then place them on others' shoulders. This may seem like it will work well, but it doesn't produce true transformation in either the leaders or those in their care.

For us as ministry leaders or as the ones being led, Jesus has some loving advice: *Whoever humbles himself will be exalted.* How paradoxical; it's the opposite of the ministry philosophy practiced by the religious leaders around Jesus and within some groups today.

Becoming humble means seeing ourselves as God sees us: needy, yet liberated. We feel the private contrition associated with our neediness, accept God's forgiveness, and then ask for help. It doesn't seem like the way to be praised. Yet in this gracious way of life, we find freedom and dignity.

Lord, sometimes it feels like someone is trying to coax
me to perform so that they look good. Yet perhaps I've done
that to others when trying to keep my own imperfection
from bugging me. This entire concept is rather fuzzy
to me. I definitely need Your help.

Make It Personal: Count the number of times you think or say the word *should* today.

Identically Wrapped Boxes

*But many . . . wept aloud . . . while
many others shouted for joy.*

Ezra 3:12

On my first morning at the cabin, I heard constant groaning, like frightened male youngsters with deepening voices. That afternoon, I heard
wildly pitched bleating sounds. Later, I discovered the llama and goat
ranch. The owner said, "My grandson will show you around."

After introducing me to all the goats, little Jeremy said, "Pudgy
sounds that way when he's annoyed. Goldenrod makes that noise when
she's happy."

"How about that strange noise the llamas make?" I asked.

"You mean their humming? Llamas don't get as annoyed or scared as
goats. But . . ." On he went about the various sounds of hungry, satisfied,
irritated, pleased animals. It made sense to him, not me. They were all fed
and treated the same way. So which animal made what sound when?

It might sound odd, but it reminded me of the Israelites' varied reactions as they rebuilt the Temple (see the book of Ezra). Some cried;
others shouted and laughed. No one responded exactly the same way,
yet each accepted the other and celebrated.

David Kiersey and Marilyn Bates, authors of *Please Understand Me*,
express it this way: "If my emotion is less than yours, or more, given the
same circumstances, try not to ask me to feel more strongly or weakly."[50]
Sometimes when we strive to worship just right, we think we need to fit
into identically wrapped praise boxes. Yet God encourages distinctive-
ness in all His creation. We can learn to lovingly receive these varied ex-
pressions of praise, as God does.

*Lord, help me accept each of
Your children's uniqueness.*

Make It Personal: Sing a silent praise song.

Enjoying My Part

There are different kinds of gifts, but the same Spirit.
1 Corinthians 12:4-7

On one of our evening dates, my husband and I enjoyed hearing our city's chamber orchestra at Symphony Hall. We listened to a piano concerto created long ago by Ludvig van Beethoven. In addition, the concert included music written by Russian composer Alfred Schnittke.

The two compositions contrasted strikingly. Beethoven's concerto blended major and minor tones with magical balance, whereas the Schnittke work introduced unfamiliar resonance and timing. Prior to the performance, the musicians placed objects on particular piano strings to alter the sound. Although the violins and violas echoed similar melodies, they were a fraction of a beat off. The result produced chuckles throughout the audience.

In both compositions, each instrument had its specific part to play. The flute didn't imitate the bassoon's sound. The cello didn't mimic the detached notes of the harpsichord. Yet the harmony captivated the audience. It worked—magnificently!

Each of us—God's children—has unique gifts and God-designed work to accomplish. It's not necessary for us to think, work or sound identically for the sake of unity. With God as our master Composer and Conductor, we can play our unique part and enjoy His brilliant creations.

Lord, I want to play my part in Your
kingdom's compositions. Help me discover my gifts
and find resources for developing them.

Make It Personal: What have you wanted to do but haven't because of what someone else might think about it? Consider investigating more about that dream. You might even write a reminder on your to-do list. Go ahead. Start the process. Enjoy!

Live and Let Live

When Jesus reached the spot, he . . . said to him,
"Zacchaeus, come down immediately. I must stay at your
house today." So he came down at once and welcomed
him gladly. All the people saw this and began to mutter.

Luke 19:5-7

"I'm seeing a Christian counselor to learn skills for coping with my chronic medical problems," shared a neighbor of mine. "My Bible study friends don't like the idea. They keep quoting Scripture, reminding me to 'have faith.' They don't understand; I'm not abandoning God. I just believe this is how He's helping me right now."

My neighbor's friends probably do want to help her, but they may not realize that their attempts to control her decisions and get her to see things their way actually increase her stress. Miriam Elliott and Susan Meltsner, coauthors of *The Perfectionist Predicament*, describe folks with this *modus operandi* as "interpersonal perfectionists." They want other people (church members, friends or relatives) to live up to specific ideals, and when others fail to do so, they feel compelled to disapprove or even shame them into agreement.

Jesus understood this dilemma. When He went to the home of an outsider—a tax collector—some disapproved and muttered. Yet Jesus didn't adopt their spiritually superior attitude or allow them to determine how He lived His life. Relying on His Father's guidance, He stayed true to His own plans, which included offering grace and acceptance to the hurting.

Lord, help me learn to live and let live.

Make It Personal: Think of a time you felt the disapproval of another person. How did it help you?

The God-shelf

But I will gain glory for myself through Pharaoh and all his
army and the Egyptians will know that I am the Lord.

Exodus 14:4

"Follow My directions," said God. "I'm going to be glorified through Pharaoh." Power-hungry Pharaoh abused the Israelites, ignoring God. When he reneged on his promise and chased after God's people, Moses brought the dilemma to God, who responded in a surprising way, at least to me. *God honored through a tyrant? Could this be?*

I think similar questions have plagued God's people for centuries. Just recently, a friend said, "I want to believe God works things for good in my life. But when the bad choices of others negatively affect me and my family, how can good come from that?"

You and I may secretly fear that the sinful actions of another person will halt the fulfillment of God's will in our own lives. However, believing that God is in charge can help to relieve our understandable anxiety. God *will* gain glory any way He wishes, even though we may not understand. Like Moses, we can trust Him.

Lord, I know I'm not responsible for another's impure
motives or actions. I wonder how You can be glorified in my unlikely
circumstances, but I'll stand back and trust You.

Make It Personal: What questionable actions of another person are weighing heavy on you? Consider putting that person and the situation on a mental "God-shelf."[51] As you do, acknowledge that God is in control of all that you place on His shelf. When your image of that person or situation starts to roll off the shelf, set it back firmly and remind yourself that they are God's job to handle.

Simple Act of Charity

Charity yields high returns.
Ecclesiastes 11:1, *THE MESSAGE*

"It was our dark, dirty and scary job to set up a musical stage on this dump site in El Salvador," said my teenage friend. "We didn't know if anyone would come, so when we finally got the lights to work, we were delighted to be surrounded by children. I noticed a little girl I'd met at the missionary's clinic earlier. 'Lord, please help this child,' I had prayed.

"As soon as we stopped singing, this same girl tugged on my shirt," continued my friend. "She tried to tell me something repeatedly. Finally, through an interpreter, I learned what she so desperately wanted me to hear. 'I'll see you later in heaven,' she said. Then this precious child joined her waiting mother and stepped out of my life. But not without making a lasting impression. That moment changed my ideas about giving, ministering and caring."

Such a contrast to the bigger-better-more-faster culture that tells us we must *do*, *know* and *spend* more in order to make a difference. My teenage friend gave up her school vacation to sing and pray with Central American children. A little girl responded with words of grateful hope. My friend told me, which inspired me to share with you.

We don't need to adopt our culture's over-the-top viewpoint in order to powerfully impact the lives of others.

You smiling yet?

Lord, I'm encouraged to know that when I share one simple act of charity, the world becomes a better place.

Make It Personal: What is one simple expression of love that you shared within the last month? Enjoy thinking about the domino effect it has had.

Personal Respite

It's useless to rise early and go to bed late, and work
your worried fingers to the bone. Don't you know he
enjoys giving rest to those he loves?

Psalm 127:2, *THE MESSAGE*

Respite became one of my favorite words during my initial recovery from perfectionism-induced workaholism and burnout. Respite: *An interval of rest and relief; a cessation for a time; a breather, recess or break; relaxation.* I wrote this definition in calligraphy on parchment paper, then framed and hung it where I could see it often. Richard and I even named our boat *Respite I,* and it soon became our simple getaway from what Jane Chesnutt, editor-in-chief at *Woman's Day* magazine, calls the "over-scheduled, over-worried, over-whatevered life."[52]

According to my Bible, Solomon wrote the words of Psalm 127:2.[53] It's part of a song, and I find it fascinating that this king, who lived a powerful bigger-better-more life, made time to scribe these song lyrics.

Our loving heavenly Father enjoys giving us respite. *How about that?* I'm wondering: Have you found a place to go and relax? A place where time is no longer a tyrant? Perhaps you've found respite under a tree in the nearby park or on the back pew of a downtown cathedral or at the corner table of the neighborhood library or kneeling over the roses in your garden or lounging on the swing on your front porch.

These "breathers" from our "over-whatevered" lives need not be elaborate, only refreshing. Claim one for yourself and celebrate the moments with God.

Lord, since You enjoy giving me rest
and respite, I accept. Thank You.

Make It Personal: What personal respite will you schedule in the next two weeks?

Turning Off the Engines

God says, "Be quiet and
know that I am God."

Psalm 46:10, *NCV*

Some of us race through the day, working, solving and worrying, and then hurry home to more projects and pressures. When our internal motors rev up, it's understandable that we have difficulty turning them off. Our heavenly Father knew that we might have a tendency to over-focus on the problems in our jobs, families, churches and world and miss the silent joy, so He said, "Be still, and know that I am God."

Current scientific research agrees that quieting the mind and body can calm the sympathetic nervous system, cause heart rate and blood pressure to drop and tense muscles to relax. Carol Turkington, author of *The Perimenopause Book*, writes, "Withdrawing from problems and calming your mind can calm the body, blunting the adrenaline surge of stress."[54]

I'm glad that God not only approves, but actually *wants* us to relax, because I just stopped working to enjoy a full-body massage. Afterward, I sat quietly for a while, breathing deeply and jotting a few prayer notes to God. What a relief to know our loving Creator thinks it's okay for us to turn off our racing internal and external engines and rest.

*Lord, I'm going to leave the race
and relax for a while.*

Make It Personal: What unnecessary burden are you carrying during your daily race? Consider putting it down. If it's something important to you (relating to your job, spouse, health or past), you can lay it down gently. It will still be there; you just won't be carrying it around any-more. Got heavy, huh?

Gaining Self-worth

The word of the Lord came to Elijah: "Go and present yourself
to Ahab." . . . When he saw Elijah, he said to him, "Is that you,
you troubler of Israel?" "I have not made trouble for Israel,"
Elijah replied. "But you and your father's family have."

1 Kings 18:1,17-18

"Is it you—the biggest troublemaker ever?" snickered King Ahab when
he saw Elijah.

"Hey, I'm not the cause of your troubles," said Elijah. Ahab blamed
Elijah for the country's problems and refused to take responsibility for
the results of his own poor choices and abusive behavior.

Some leaders, like Ahab, blame others (even the ones in their care)
for their self-made problems. Sadly, perhaps in an effort to minimize
their own toxic shame and legitimate guilt, they try hard to convince
themselves and everyone else that the truth-teller is the problem. Yet
noticing or verbalizing a problem does not make you the problem.

It's acceptable to speak about what feels abusive to you. When you
and I accept responsibility for our own actions and choices, we breathe
hope back into our suffocating lives. We all (both the blamer and the
blame-ee) gain a sense of self-worth when we become accountable for
our decisions and growth. Then we're able to fulfill our God-given roles
with grace-filled integrity. Positive personal change becomes an exciting possibility when we stop "passing the buck."

Lord, this is a little confusing to me still.
Please give me clarity. I want to be free.

Make It Personal: When do you give your personal God-given power
away? To whom? When?

I'm Not Crazy

Overwork makes for restless sleep.
Ecclesiastes 5:3, *THE MESSAGE*

Am I making too much of culture's bigger-better-more-faster craze? I didn't think so, but I wanted verification. "The world is now producing nearly two exabytes of new and unique information per year," writes Kevin A. Miller, author of *Surviving Information Overload*. "Don't feel bad if you don't know what an exabyte is. No one does. It's a new term, one they had to coin for a billion gigabytes." Miller maintains that "there are 260,000 billboards, 11,520 newspapers, 11,556 periodicals, 27,000 video outlets, 40,000 new book titles, and 60,000,000,000 pieces of junk mail every year" for us to choose from, read, compare, manage and heed.[55]

An emergent group of "information environmentalists" states that their objective is to reclaim mental respite from the constant barrage of cell phones, personal digital assistants, instant messaging, email, specialized cable channels and massive amounts of news, entertainment and sales pitches.[56] "It feels to me that as a result of the high speed at which we're operating . . . we're kind of numbing ourselves. Just trying to get by," says Dr. David Levy, professor at University of Washington's Information School and researcher at a think-tank that created the personal computer and laser printer.[57]

So I'm *not* crazy when I get the gut-sickening sensation that I'll never catch up! I won't. Nobody can. Thus, be gone unnecessary guilt! I'm headed for fewer sleepless nights trying to figure out how to get it all done.

Lord, I can't maneuver through this
over-the-top mania alone. We're a team and
I'm grateful. That's enough for me today.

Make It Personal: What's your take on this information?

Head Held High

How blessed is the man who has made the Lord his trust;
and has not turned . . . to those who lapse into falsehood.

Psalm 40:4, *NASB*

"You shouldn't feel that way" or "You're not tired. Your sister still has energy" or "We can't stop for a bathroom break now. You don't have to go that bad, anyway" or even "You should pray like your cousin does."

Comments like these may sound familiar. Perhaps you have been shamed into doubting your emotions, perceptions, desires or needs, causing you to lose your sense of individuality. "Each of us is surrounded by external sources of shame. These vary, of course," write David Johnson and Jeff VanVonderen in *The Subtle Power of Spiritual Abuse*. "Families where people are called names or compared, or where parents have their needs met by the performance of the children, instill messages of shame in their members."[58] The authors contend that even billboards, magazine ads and television commercials shame us by promising ways to make us more valuable, lovable or capable.

As wise women of God, we can cease sacrificing who we are for the sake of another's ego-needs or our own desire for protection from negative reaction. Although God has unlimited power, He never victimizes us to prove it. Instead, He treats us with respect and love. He's worth trusting—even imperfectly.

Lord, I think I've allowed others to make my decisions
for me. I don't want to do that anymore. Please help
me give up my victim mentality so that I can walk
with my head high and my heart focused on You.

Make It Personal: Name a time you felt respected and loved. What was happening?

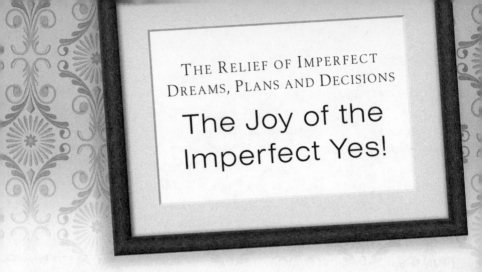

The Joy of the Imperfect Yes!

Sometimes we strive too hard to make our dreams and plans turn out just right and say yes to tasks God hasn't asked us to do. Or we say yes to what God *has* called us to do and then adopt unrealistic expectations for how it will play out. Yet when we say yes to partnering with God, He doesn't expect us to do or be it all—perfectly.

Things don't always turn out as planned after we say, "Yes, I'll take that job" or "Yes, I'll marry you and become a mother" or "Yes, I'll do that project." On the morning of our annual Webb Invitational Golf Tournament, Richard announced, "The garage door broke." With the tournament starting in 1 hour and 60 people coming for dinner on our patio, we needed a repairman ASAP. Reaching for the phonebook, Richard knocked over a large glass bottle, which crashed and sent shards everywhere. I sent Richard and our houseguest ahead, left a message for the repairman, cleaned up the glass and gooey puddles, and then headed to the golf course.

We soon discovered that we were given the wrong tee-time, which bummed us out because it threw off our schedule. Finally, the repairman called back, I met him at the house, and he fixed the door—eventually. After pressing the button inside the garage, I jumped to miss the sensor, banged into the descending garage door and dropped to the ground in pain. I felt my head. No blood, so I stumbled to the car and returned to the golf course.

The irony is that we had prepared meticulously for this event for an entire year. Yet all that careful planning didn't halt these irritating surprises.

If we expect that because we work hard we will know guaranteed success, or that because we give much we'll be wealthy, or that because we eat well and take care of our bodies we'll never be sick, then we're certainly headed for some disappointing shockers. We live in a world where the future isn't always predictable or controllable. Our carefully designed plans and dreams may not come to fruition as we hope or pray.

"Yes, Lord. I'll go where You want and do what You've designed for me," I prayed after months of inner prodding. Full of purpose, I prepared for ministry, enrolled in Bible school, married and lived out my pastor's-wife dream for 12 years. Then Richard told me that he had decided to leave his ministry position. My dream shattered into a thousand sharp pieces within my soul. I hated the pain, denied my disappointment, surmised that God had changed His mind, and ran head-long into business. Seven years later, I collapsed and burned. *I didn't plan this. What happened?*

Imperfect life happened, just as it did for those who shared their stories in *The Relief of Imperfection*: Teresa said, "With the good, I'll always have some messiness. This actually brings me relief." Brigita wrote, "I've relaxed the unrealistic expectation that I must be perfect in order to be loved by a man." Jen shared, "We didn't get our perfect baby dream fulfilled, yet God did what was best for us." Kelli wrote, "Although I had the perfect dream [to be a stay-at-home mom], God had a different vision." Cheryl shared, "I can't compare myself to others. They finished [college] sooner, but I took 17 years and had valid reasons. What I previously used to berate myself with is precisely what God used to love and encourage me now." Sarah (who tragically lost her husband) wrote, "We miss Gino. Yet everything—my marriage, our life together, our children and his illness—are all wrapped up in the decisions I made. To regret one means the others wouldn't have been." Nick (born without arms or legs) shared, "No matter how your dreams or plans are crushed, God knows you and cares."[59]

Sometimes circumstances become sadly perplexing. Still, in the midst of inevitable imperfection and because of God's loving grace, we can learn to say yes (and no!) with confident relief. Our dreams, plans and choices don't have to be perfect to be fulfilling and God-honoring.

Learning to Flex

Don't brag about what will happen tomorrow.
You don't really know what will happen then.

Proverbs 27:1, *NCV*

I had great expectations for my day. However, before I could leave the house, the phone rang numerous times, delaying my start. It rained during my drive, slowing my travel time. The motel where I had made reservations was filled with high school athletes, so I hunted for different accommodations. When I finally found a vacancy, they gave me an outside room in a dark alley. It was sub-zero weather and I was alone and had requested an inside room, so I asked to be moved. I dropped the key to my new room down a crevice in my van and spent half an hour trying to retrieve it.

Meanwhile, my growling stomach reminded me that I hadn't eaten. On the way to the restaurant, traffic snarled to a stop. Two police cars and an ambulance blocked the intersection. A wreck! Another delay! *This is not how I planned it!*

I can make detailed intentional plans, but I can't *guarantee* the outcome. (Hey, I *know* this, but with my tendency to try too hard to make all my strategies and dreams come out just right, I have to remind myself often.) And when I listen, admit my disappointment, adjust my expectations and accept doable options, the knot in my stomach usually relaxes. Then I'm ready to enjoy myself and others.

Lord, sometimes things don't go the way I intended.
When that happens, help me learn to flex.

Make It Personal: What isn't turning out the way you planned? Name two or three options you might consider. Now take a deep breath. What will you do next?

In the End

*In this world you will have trouble. But take heart!
I have overcome the world.*

John 16:33

Several years ago, I worked with a painting sub-contractor on a large renovation job. At the end of one particularly stressful day, he stopped by my office to chat. "You know, I'm a Christian now, and I don't understand why God keeps allowing all these problems to invade my business. Delays, missed deadlines, broken equipment, injuries, trucking strikes, agitated clients and disgruntled employees. What's the deal?"

Yeah, what is the deal, anyway? It's tempting to conclude that we're doing something wrong if and when we get hit with problems. That's quite an uncomfortable predicament for anyone who believes everything must be just right.

But Jesus said that problems are an inevitable part of life in this imperfect world. Life wasn't always pleasant for Him. And neither are we, His followers, exempt from hurt, disappointment, rejection and frustration. Normally the daily problems we face aren't the end of the world. Yet, even if they did bring the end, we would see Jesus face to face. *Either way, we win.*

*Lord, the unpleasant daily circumstances in my
life normally aren't unbearable. When my knee-jerk
reaction is to panic, help me to remember this fact, ask for
Your help, work toward a reasonable solution and then
move forward. My ultimate hope is in You.*

Make It Personal: What problems are frustrating you? List your day-to-day dilemmas in one column and your life- or faith-threatening ones in another column. What do you observe from your lists?

Lessening Your Anxiety

They were terrified. But he said to them, "It is I; don't be afraid."

John 6:19-20

After rowing nearly four miles from shore, they notice a man approaching them—walking on the water! It is night time, a storm rocks their boat, and now *this*. What's going on? How can someone defy nature and walk on water? Terror grips them. Jesus sees their panic and immediately eases it. When they discover that the Man walking on the water is Jesus, their fear evaporates.

Like the disciples, you and I often fear what we don't understand. Perplexed by your best friend's emotional and mental problems? Frightened at your spouse's diagnosis and your own coping skills? Anxious and confused about your child's choices? Terrified of facing how your past pain is affecting you now? When we just don't *get* what's happening, we may feel out of control. That's scary. So sometimes we mock or devalue what we cannot comprehend.

What do you have a difficult time understanding and consequently fear? Take action today. Go to the library. Read about the subject. Call an expert. Ask responsible questions. Pray for insight. Listen and learn. Knowledge may not completely eradicate the fear, as it did when Jesus stepped into the boat with His disciples, but gaining understanding certainly can lessen your anxiety.

Lord, I believe that You don't want me to remain anxious about what I don't understand. Please help me discover the facts and reduce my confusion.

Make It Personal: What frightens or confuses you about one of your dreams, plans or choices? Choose two of the options above, discover pertinent information and increase your understanding.

No Hiding

And since we have gifts that differ according to the grace
given to us, let each exercise them accordingly.

Romans 12:6, *NASB*

*If shame causes a person to hide who she is, I must be ashamed of myself. I hide
the books I read for fear of being ridiculed. I practice piano only when no one is
around. I refrain from sharing my thoughts when they differ from someone who
doesn't understand me. I'm afraid I'll be considered arrogant if I do what I believe God is calling me to do.*

Years ago, I wrote these words in my journal. Reading them now, I
feel sad because these fears kept me, for quite some time, from becoming the person God created me to be. I've met other women (and men!)
beset by such troubling self-views, so I recognize that it is possible for
any of us to feel ashamed simply by being ourselves.

Here's what I'm learning: Just because a friend or relative is not a
musician doesn't mean I can't be. I can enjoy reading, studying and
teaching even though another person would rather do a hands-on helping project. If someone I love participates in sports and I don't, that's
all right.

They can use the talent and gifts God gave them and pursue the activities and ministries they enjoy. And I can do the same. God wants us
to celebrate our differences.

*Lord, please help me to accept my personality
characteristics and talents as gifts from You. And when
someone else doesn't understand who and what I am,
give me courage to smile and not hide.*

Make It Personal: What do you enjoy doing? How can you do more of
what you like?

Unique Calling

Moses thought that his own people would realize that God
was using him to rescue them, but they did not.

Acts 7:25

When I read Katie Brazelton's book, *Conversations on Purpose for Women*, one of her thought-provoking questions particularly left an impression on me: *What's your motive for serving?* I simply responded, "God asked me to and I said yes." I believe that God called me to join Him in His work on earth. I even wrote a high school paper titled "Living My Dream in Christian Service."[60]

Although it hasn't always been this way, I'm now living out God's calling on my life as a writer, Bible teacher, speaker and life coach. I've met numerous women who also sense God calling them to Christian service. Invariably, these committed women wish their loved ones—usually their husbands—would recognize this calling and support and share their mission. When their loved ones don't, the indifference and/or rejection the women feel leaves them hurt and disappointed. I understand.

The liberating truth is that others, even those closest to us, have the right *not* to share our burden for ministry. The call or passion is ours, not theirs. Our responsibility includes being compassionate, open and honest with those we love; true to the principles or ministry we feel strongly about; and patient with God's overall plan. As we believe this, we're free to love and serve joyously.

Lord, I'm responsible for my own calling before You.
I won't impose that call on anyone else.

Make It Personal: What is God asking you to do? (Consider reading the story in Acts 7 of Moses' calling and how others responded.)

Grace Notes

If you hold anything against anyone, forgive him.
Mark 11:25

For years, I put myself in an impossible position by trying to be perfect all the time. I silently shamed myself, expected too much, crushed creativity and robbed myself of nourishment, fun, sleep and relaxation while trying to please others and do everything just right. I let anger turn to resentment, stuffed it down and became depressed. I wronged myself, others and God in the process.

One morning during my recovery from burnout, I realized that the one person I most needed to forgive was myself. I wrote in my journal: *I've harmed you, Joan. I'm sorry. I'll try to be kinder and more forgiving now. It's okay for you to nurture yourself and become the person God designed you to be.* God wants us to have compassionate hearts toward all people, ourselves included.

Last night while editing the two previous paragraphs, I thought, *There's something more here.* I tried to find it. Browsing through books, commentaries, my notes and the Bible, it eluded me—so I went to bed. This morning when I awoke, I looked at the clock: *7:30 A.M.! I did it again!* For two weeks, I've overslept until 7:00 or 7:30, when usually I'm up by 5:30. And all week I had been asking, *What's wrong with you, Joan?*

In that moment, God whispered, "Grace!"

Really?

"Like musical grace notes, Joan—the lovely extra sounds in an ordinary song, put in 'just because.' Nothing's *wrong*. Just enjoy the added-on rest."

Forgiving relief: the grace notes of God. Enjoy!

Lord, I'm just so grateful.

Make It Personal: This week look for God's grace notes to you.

Moving Close

When Simon Peter saw this, he fell at Jesus' knees
and said, "Go away from me, Lord; I am a sinful man!"
For he and all his companions were astonished at the catch
of fish they had taken. . . . Then Jesus said to Simon,
"Don't be afraid; from now on you will catch men."

Luke 5:8,10

Exhausted and discouraged from fishing all night with no success, Simon and his crew decided to take Jesus' suggestion, even though it seemed pointless. They tried again. Immediately, fish came from seemingly nowhere. They signaled another boat. Filled to the brim with the catch, both boats started to sink with the weight of so many fish.

An amazed Simon Peter begged, "Lord, please get out of here. I'm not good enough for You."

"Don't worry, Peter," said Jesus. "From now on, you'll be working with Me."

Some of us, like Peter, focus on our failures and withdraw. "Be assured that the voices of shame and self-condemnation that speak in our minds with such harshness are not of God," writes Marsha Crockett in her book *Break Through*. "These voices are the illusions others have spoken into us. When we accept what they say as the complete truth about ourselves, they keep us from God."[61]

Peter feared getting close to Jesus because he listened to a faulty inner message. Yet Jesus calmed his fears with words of assurance: "Don't be afraid to get to know Me and trust Me. I have a plan. We'll work together, and it'll be just fine."

Lord, like You did for Peter,
please calm my self-doubt.

Make It Personal: Take a step toward God today. He's right there.

Redeeming Time

Redeeming the time.
Ephesians 5:16, *KJV*

As a young Christian, I memorized this verse: "Redeeming the time, be-cause the days are evil." "Redeeming time," I surmised, meant that I must make each 24-hour day of my entire life productive—so that's what I determined to do.

Occasionally I paused enough to notice that *time* was controlling *me*, rather than me redeeming time. I then resolved to adjust, only to be sucked up again into excessive doing. I thought that if I perfectly re-deemed my time, I could accomplish much and God would be pleased.

Vonda Skelton, author of *Seeing Through the Lies*, writes, "I've inad-vertently adopted the philosophy that says I must produce every minute of every day, that my worth is tied to my busyness and that my value is defined by my production."[62] Vonda and I both have discovered that this is not only a misconception but also an impossibility. In her book, Vonda concludes that God doesn't require us to sacrifice our lives on the altar of busyness in pursuit of the impossible. Speeding through life is not a useful way to fulfill our God-given dreams.

I tried so hard to fill each waking minute with worthwhile activity and accomplishment. A better way to redeem life's opportunities—and the way God had in mind in the first place—is to relax, be ourselves (that's doable!) and enjoy the work He has given us to do. Sometimes I practice this; sometimes I don't. Still, God knows my desire to effec-tively and patiently redeem my time.

Lord, what's up for me today?
Let's do it together.

Make It Personal: Consider praying the above prayer each day this week and then listening for God's personal response to you.

Ordinary Stuff

Jesus . . . saw a tax collector by the name of Levi sitting at this
tax booth. "Follow me," Jesus said . . . and Levi . . . followed him.

Luke 5:27-28

"When asked what my husband does, I change the subject," said a
friend. "People don't understand how anyone could be a tax auditor."
Long ago, tax collectors had even less respect than they do today. People
viewed tax collector Levi (also called Matthew), with contempt, yet
Jesus chose him to be on His 12-man team.

Although I hesitate to admit this, at times I've made silent judgments
about who is or is not spiritually mature. With the help of a
couple of accountability partners, though, I'm becoming increasingly
accepting of myself and others. It helps to remember that God is more
interested in a person's willingness and faith than whether they make
faultless decisions or produce perfect plans. Oswald Chambers, author
of *My Utmost for His Highest*, wrote, "The men and women our Lord
sends out on His enterprises are the ordinary human stuff."[63]

I've noticed that some women think they'll never be good enough
for God to use in His work, while others believe they have proved themselves
to be extraordinary and He *must* utilize them and their talents.
However, God doesn't say, "You're super-human; I'll call you" or "She's
always right; I'll send her." God employs the ordinary people of this
world—like you and me.

Lord, I'm not perfect, yet You choose
to work in my life. I love that!

Make It Personal: What silent judgments have you made in the past?
How did they help?

Internal Change

*And then take on an entirely new way of life—a God-fashioned life,
a life renewed from the inside and working itself into your conduct
as God accurately reproduces his character in you.*
Ephesians 4:23-24, *THE MESSAGE*

I went to a motel with the sole purpose of working, studying and writing for four uninterrupted days. After working for several hours, I decided to take a real meal break and not just snack at my desk—or go without. (That decision alone was a triumph for me.) However, preparing to go downstairs to the cafe, I felt the urge to take a book so that I could do more research while eating, thereby making "the best use of my time." Instead, I went to dinner empty-handed, sat quietly, relaxed, ate my dinner and then returned, refreshed, to my room to work.

Then, because I had chosen fried fish for dinner (I don't usually order fried foods), I had an upset stomach. Not too pleasant. Yet previously, I would have berated myself for making such a poor menu choice. This time I heard my internal voice saying, *It's okay, Joan. This won't last forever.*

Later that evening, I realized that I'd forgotten to schedule the guest speaker for an upcoming event I had agree to plan. I didn't panic. Instead, I called a fellow board member and asked for assistance.

We *can* change—from the inside out.

*Lord, thank You for simple reminders
that with Your help, I am changing.*

Make It Personal: How is your life changing? On this page or in your journal, jot down evidences of God "reproducing His character" in you. Read the above verse again and celebrate.

Life Isn't Perfect

The LORD is my strength and my shield; my heart trusted
in Him, and I am helped; therefore my heart greatly rejoices,
and with my song I will praise Him.

Psalm 28:7, *NKJV*

Richard and I attended a celebration concert featuring the compositions of Petr Eben of Czechoslovakia. Many works of this talented composer and musician had never before been performed in the United States due to the restrictions and censorship of the communist government.

A talented young Eben consistently practiced and performed the music he loved, fully expecting to pursue his musical education and passion without interruption. Yet everything changed when he was thrown into the concentration camp at Buchenwald during the war. Obviously, this was not his plan. He witnessed unspeakable horror and feared for his life. Even after being released, he lived through a further 40 years of political oppression. As a result of his life experiences, Eben's sacred compositions reflect both the joy *and* the pain, the peace *and* the struggle of human existence.

About his musical work, the Suita balladica for cello and piano, he said, "Faith and hope cannot be killed, the spirit cannot be defeated by external events."[64] If we expect that we'll experience our dreams in just the way we plan, prepare and picture them, we may find ourselves shocked and disappointed. In this imperfect world, our tomorrows are not always controllable. Our meticulously strategized plans may not work out as we hope. Our most passionate dreams may not materialize as we envision. Life is not perfect. Only God is—and that is certain. Petr Eben realized this, and it sustained him during the difficult times.

Lord, You're my hope amidst unfulfilled dreams
and confusing situations.

Make It Personal: How does acknowledging that life isn't perfect and that your dreams and plans aren't guaranteed bring you relief?

Confronting Unreasonable Fear

*Be careful, keep calm and don't be afraid. Do not lose heart
because of these two smoldering stubs of firewood . . .
the Sovereign LORD says: "It will not take place."*

Isaiah 7:4,7

"I'm afraid of that big dog, Mom," said my client's little boy. "He might get me."

"Timmy, we'll be careful," his mom replied. "Walk between Joan and me." We continued past the dog to my office.

"Hello," said the collie's owner, whom I knew. He and the dog played catch with a small ball. Timmy watched cautiously.

"They're having fun," he said, relaxing his grip on his mom's arm.

"You want to throw the ball?" asked the dog's owner. Soon my client's little guy joined the fun, playing with the dog he had previously feared.

This experience holds significant meaning for me. I've realized that although some of my fears are legitimate, others prove irrational and rob me of the joy of living. Like my client's son, when I wisely observe and then move in closer toward my fear, I often discover that it wasn't like I thought at all.

If I'm afraid of someone's reaction because I think I might sound foolish or do something wrong, I back off. This behavior often keeps me from enjoying another person's company—and sometimes limits the intimacy I desire. Yet when I challenge my fear, staying true to my own personality, beliefs and values, I usually find that I was safe all along.

*Lord, please give me courage to challenge my
unreasonable fear. I know that You are in control.*

Make It Personal: Think of a time you worried about someone or something and it turned out fine. What did you take away from the experience?

Out of the Abundance

Taking the five loaves and the two fish . . . he gave thanks. . . .
Then he gave them to the disciples, and the disciples gave them
to the people. They all ate and were satisfied, and the disciples
picked up twelve basketfuls . . . that were left over.

Matthew 14:19-20

I hesitate to admit this, but I've had a tendency to ration my generosity. Under outer layers of genuine caring, I've been afraid that if I give unreservedly to others, there won't be any left for me. Perhaps it's because I've equated loving with having no limits on what I do for others and rarely saying no. I misguidedly believed that to be an ideal 1 Corinthians 13 woman, I must abandon my own insights and ministry to prove that I am patient, kind and unselfish.[65]

Paradoxically, this hindered my ability to love as I longed to do. I truly needed to retrieve what was rightfully mine—my perceptions, gifts and individuality. Then I could risk giving generously out of the abundance of who God created me to be.

When Jesus provided food for more than 5,000 people, inviting them to eat all they wanted, He still had 12 baskets left over. Jesus, liberal with His compassionate concern, didn't ration for fear that being generous would deplete His resources. Like Jesus, we can be generous without relinquishing who we are, and care while maintaining our God-given identities.

Lord, I don't wish to be stingy. Help me give
out of the overflow of who You made me to be.

Make It Personal: What is inherently yours that you've given away and need to retrieve?

Turning On the Light

*Where does understanding dwell? . . . God understands
the way to it and he alone knows where it dwells.*

Job 28:20,23

After driving home from a date one night, my son—a teenager at the time—realized that he'd lost his billfold. He hunted in his pockets, the car, his room and throughout the house. He searched the driveway and yard, but in the dark it was difficult to see. Eventually he gave up and flopped in bed, perturbed and tired.

In the sunlight the next morning, he found his wallet in the yard, exactly where he had looked the previous night. Although pleased, he also felt annoyed that he had wasted so much time and energy looking without success the night before.

Perhaps you experience similar thoughts and emotions when searching for knowledge, insight and wisdom to make effective decisions and to fulfill your God-given dreams. I have. It can be frustrating. Yet when light shines on a lost or confusing issue or problem, it *is* easier to see and understand. While we're in the dark, our frantic searching remains futile.

We would do well to step back, relax and wait until God illumines our path with light and understanding. Then we can move forward with joy-filled confidence and intentionality.

*Lord, all insight originates with You. You are the
source of understanding, good judgment and wisdom.
Please turn on the light for me.*

Make It Personal: Jot down what's confusing you right now. Now write what you already know about the situation. What's still missing? Ask God to fill this gap with insight and wisdom. Then relax and wait for the light to dawn.

Scooting Fear Out the Door

There is no fear in love—dread does not exist;
but full-grown (complete, perfect) love turns fear out of
doors and expels every trace of terror!

1 John 4:18, *AMP*

The bride snuggles close to her husband. The picture appears peaceful, yet deep inside, the young woman wrestles with questions: *What should I say? What must I do to make him happy? How can I assure he'll be pleased with me and our marriage?* Love and commitment? Yes. Relaxed enjoyment? Not really. Something's disturbing the newlywed dream.

This bride is me. I thought that to be a godly wife, I needed to strive constantly, give and never take, work hard and keep silent—as if a successful husband-wife relationship was all up to me. Tears rim my eyes as I write this now. I loved Richard when I said yes and I love him now, but sometimes I allow fear to taint that love. I don't want it to.

Years ago I read that "there is no fear in genuine love," so I took the first uneasy step to seek help. I have grown to be less obsessed with Richard's response to me (and that's good!). We enjoy mutual respect and a sense of teamwork (and I'm grateful!). I know that I will not love perfectly here on earth, yet I've decided to cease striving and cherish both the human and divine love offered to me.

Lord, fear has held such terror for me. When the
old ineffective pattern threatens, help me scoot fear
out the door and welcome love in.

Make It Personal: Read the above verse again. When have you turned fear out of doors in your relationships?

My Fluctuating Best

I have learned the secret of being content in
any and every situation, whether well fed or hungry,
whether living in plenty or in want.

Philippians 4:12

Sometimes when preparing for a teaching assignment, the right ideas, activities and examples refuse to come. I hustle all day, even several days, knowing I haven't done my best work. Mediocre stuff is all I seem to create. When this happens, I have a choice—actually, I have several choices. I can become frustrated, quit and get behind schedule. I can obsess and spend painstaking hours on one or two points until my eyes cross and my shoulders spasm. Or I can choose to keep working steadily whether I think the result is superb or not.

The following simple comments from Melody Beattie's book, *The Language of Letting Go,* help me be more accepting during these frustrating times: "There are days when our best is less than we hoped for. Let those times go too. Start over tomorrow. Work things through, until our best becomes better."[66]

Like Paul, sometimes our best results in poverty, other times in prosperity. Learning to be content with both our best performances and our could-have-been-better times will lessen our anxiety and help us live more peaceful and accepting lives.

Lord, I realize I can only do my best at any
given moment, since that's all that's available to me at
that time. Help me, as Paul did, to learn the secret of
being content with my fluctuating "best."

Make It Personal: When are you too hard on yourself? When are you too hard on your circumstances? Consider adapting Paul's secret as your own.

Pleasing God/Enjoying Life

"For I know the plans I have for you," declares the Lord,
"plans to prosper you and not to harm you, plans to give you hope
and a future. . . . Pray to me, and I will listen."

Jeremiah 29:11

Sometimes we get the idea that we need to stay unhappy or confused in order to please God. Recently I heard statements like these from three different people:

- "I need to declare a major so I can plan my schedule, but I'm confused. I *want* to be an engineer, but maybe God thinks I should do something else."
- "I've been offered a great position here in town. I like it and it seems to fit me. You think God minds if I accept?"
- "Brandon asked me to be his wife. We've prayed about it, love one another and share similar goals. Yet I'm worried. Maybe God doesn't want me to be married."

God wants us to trust Him and enjoy our lives. He's a wise, caring Father who delights neither in depriving us or keeping us forever guessing. Although we won't always make picture-perfect choices, God won't frown on us if we make decisions that seem favorable to us at the time. Augustine said, "Love God, and do as you please." Indeed, God desires that we cease fretting and start living in the fullness of His rich plans for us.

Lord, sometimes I get confused about my future.
Please guide my decisions.

Make It Personal: God's plans for us are usually in harmony with our natural talents and interests. How can that confidence help you with your current decisions?

Claiming Joy

"But what about you?" [Jesus] asked.

Matthew 16:15

"How do you feel about God?" asked a concerned neighbor.

"Oh, I never think about it," said the man. "My wife takes care of all that for me."

My mother was the concerned neighbor in this conversation, years ago, and she shared it with me. It made such an impression on my young mind that I never forgot it. It reminds me of when Jesus asked His disciples to tell Him who people said He was. "Some say You're a prophet," they answered. "Others say You're John the Baptist or Elijah."

"What about you?" asked Jesus. "Who do *you* say I am?" This simple, personal question deserved a straight answer and Peter responded, "You're the Christ, the Messiah."

I find it incredibly sad that some people, like the man who talked with my mom, choose not to accept responsibility for their own beliefs or growth. Perhaps when they were youngsters, someone made their spiritual and emotional decisions for them and it just seemed easier to keep relegating the job to another person. (Sometimes the over-helpers are willing to step in at this point.)

Yet the truth is that spiritual, emotional and mental growth requires that each person make her own choices. It isn't possible to live effectively through someone else's perceptions, beliefs or prayers. Just as Peter and the other disciples had, you and I have the privilege of deciding for ourselves. Accepting personal responsibility, taking intentional action and experiencing the resulting transformation breed self-respect. Then you and I have joy to claim.

Lord, I really want to take responsibility for my own development—regardless of what anyone else does or says.

Make It Personal: What decision has upped your self-respect?

Eliminating Miserable Misbeliefs

Thus the people were divided because of Jesus.
Some wanted to seize him.

John 7:43-44

I'm amazed by Jesus. His work on the cross makes me right with God, and His life example in the midst of imperfection and disappointment shows me how to live. For instance, many loved Jesus; others loathed Him. But that didn't stop Jesus from fulfilling His purpose in life. He seemed unsurprised by it all. Although He cared about others, their opinions didn't alter his plans.

I've discovered a misbelief guaranteed to make me (and you!) miserable: *In order to be happy, I must be loved by everybody.* Obviously, this isn't a belief that Jesus espoused. When adhering to this misconception, we try too hard to guarantee everyone's love and appreciation. We may give in even though to do so conflicts with our values. Or we may attempt to control others' reactions to us by hedging the truth. Sometimes we're shocked and upset when someone else doesn't believe as we do and react as we would.

Not everyone loved and agreed with Jesus; not all will love and agree with us. This isn't surprising. But by fulfilling our God-given dream and purposes, we can live satisfying and significant lives, regardless of the reactions of those around us. We don't have to be loved and appreciated by everyone to be happy and content.

*Lord, it's a relief to know that I can be who You made
me to be even though others may disagree with me. Please help
me to be courageous and consistent.*

Make It Personal: What inspires you about the way Jesus lived His life in this flawed world?

A Backward Process

When I was in great need, he saved me. Be at rest
once more, O my soul, for the LORD has been good to you.

Psalm 116:6

Finding it difficult to balance a demanding work schedule with the rest of my over-active life, my insides churned. I fought off the confusing thoughts and emotions—in vain. Finally, I called my friend Sue. We both were committed to reducing the trying-too-hard-to-make-it-all-just-right Christian superwoman approach to life that we had been taught. After listening to my rambling and making a few suggestions, she reflected, "Well, Joan, it seems we still attempt to figure it all out *first*, with all the right words and responses, before we share our need and ask for help."

I guess so. It's as if we believe that we dare not admit our confusion and angst until we understand it better, know what to call it and how to explain it. We have the process backward. God wants to help us *now*. A hopeful future becomes more than wishful thinking when we accept God's intervention in our lives today. God comforts, supports, cares, loves and saves us *in* our need. Even before we know what the exact problem is, we can seek God's help. Today.

Lord, I don't know how to explain myself.
But I need You. I'm confused about my dreams, plans
and purposes. So I'm asking for help now, instead of
waiting until I have it all figured out.

Make It Personal: Stop. Right now. It doesn't matter what you don't know yet. Ask God for help and let your soul be at rest.

More Than a Label

The disciples were called Christians first at Antioch.

Acts 11:26

"When I was a child," said my friend, "the aunt who helped raise me used the word 'Christian' as a whip to keep me in line. She often said, 'This is the Christian way to act,' when she wanted me to do something for her or make her look good. Then, when she didn't agree with one of my ideas or decisions—or someone else's, for that matter—she said, 'That's not the Christian thing to do!' Because of my aunt's attitude, I vowed that I would never allow myself to be labeled 'Christian.'"

Some of us associate the word "Christian" with a long list of dos and don'ts or with a system of shame and blame. Like my friend, we may need to reprogram our childhood tapes to accept the true meaning of this word. Being a Christian is not merely something we *do*; it is *who we are*. In fact, the word was first coined as a noun, not an adjective. People called Peter and the others "Christians" because they followed God's Son, Jesus Christ, and pursued a relationship with Him. The word means "Christ's follower." Becoming a Christian—deciding to believe and join in partnership with Jesus—is a liberating life choice.

Lord Jesus, I back off when anyone defines my relationship
with You as a set of shoulds and musts. Bearing the
title of Christian is a graceful privilege. Help me pass to
others the mercy and benevolence of Your name.

Make It Personal: Jot down some practical ways that your relationship with Jesus has impacted your dreams, plans and decisions.

Striving Too Hard Dulls Your Soul

While facilitating a women's retreat in Georgia's lush green mountains, I reunited with a long-lost hobby: knitting. I'd forgotten how to cast on and stitch, so during our free afternoon, I asked the teacher to show me again. After knitting several rows, the instructor said to the other knitters, "Wow, look at Joan. She's holding the yarn and needles so loosely you can see holes between the stitches."

Whoa, that's a switch-er-roo, I thought as I recalled my previous squeeze-it-'til-it's-perfect knitting attempts. In my effort to complete a beautifully flawless project (whether a baby dress, a pair of mittens, a muffler or whatever), I'd hold the needles and yarn so tightly that each new row shriveled up smaller than the last. Not pretty. Yet I heard the teacher continue, "Way to go, Joan. Your relaxed knitting looks great on this scarf project."

It reminded me of when my husband returned from a "surprisingly good" (his words) golf game and said, "Today I decided to play it easy. At each tee I said, 'So what?' to myself and hit the ball. It sailed down the fairway. I even putted well. Seems when I stopped trying to manipulate the course, I relaxed and played better." (*Interesting*, I thought, so I researched online and sure enough, golfers often sabotage their games by trying so hard they tense their muscles and thwart their progress.)

Trying too hard to knit just right dulls the finished product. Trying too hard to hit a perfect shot dulls your golf game. And trying too hard in your spiritual life—to achieve flawless prayer and quiet times, to acquire impressive amounts of biblical wisdom and become a perfectly dedicated Christian—can dull your soul.

Perhaps Peter tried too hard to appear perfectly faithful when he said, "I will lay down my life for You, Jesus." A few days later, his I'll-do-this-just-right spirituality backfired and he disowned his Lord (see John 13:37-38). Even John the Baptist, Jesus' God-appointed "prep-man," experienced less-than-perfect faith days. While in prison (didn't anyone care?), John said to his friends, "Go ask Jesus if He's the one God promised, or if we should keep looking" (see Matthew 11:2-11). I find it fascinating (and relief-producing) that John's doubt didn't embarrass him into silence. He took his questions to Jesus. And Jesus didn't shame him into improved faith and spirituality. In fact, He honored John by calling him a great man who had fulfilled his God-given mission.

Recently, I tried a new tactic with myself. Instead of asking, "What am I doing wrong, Lord?" as usual (which can lure me into the numb-and-number, dulled-soul void), I asked, "Lord, what am I doing right?" It was a truly difficult exercise for me, because I've been conditioned to look for the negative. (*Isn't that the only way I'll grow?*) The first time I asked the "doing right" question, God surprised me with His response, which took me back to Jesus' encouraging statements after John's questions. Although there were no "greatest woman" comments, He did whisper to my spirit: "Doing right, Joan? Talking with Me throughout your day. Saying yes when I ask you to do something. Releasing other people's decisions to Me. Cooperating to become the you I created." Amazing, huh?

Yet I'm not perfect. (Shock!) I just spent four hours trying to squeeze the life out of these last two paragraphs. I'm not kidding. This entire morning, I didn't catch on that I was trying too hard to make this section's introduction just right. So here's my conclusion: Whether you're feeling numb or elated and wondering how to approach Jesus, remember His response to Cousin John—and to me. Jesus greets our honest comments, questions and interaction with spiritual positivity, validation and love. So we can stop trying so hard to be perfect Christian women. That makes me smile. How about you?

Without Ceasing?

*Rejoice always, pray without ceasing, in everything give thanks;
for this is the will of God in Christ Jesus for you.*

1 Thessalonians 5:17, *NKJV*

One morning, I overheard a minister say, "The only time I don't feel any stress is when I pray." Perhaps Paul realized when he wrote the words "pray without ceasing" that the simple, intentional act of honest prayer was anxiety reducing.

But what does this verse really mean? Did Paul really think we ought to spend our entire day kneeling at a prayer altar or locked in our closet? Is this admonition merely another angst-producing *should* to fulfill?

We could possibly liken our praying to eating or sleeping. Most of us sleep every day, but at the appropriate times. We don't always have a mouth full of food, yet we eat on a regular or continual basis. To stop eating or sleeping would bring disastrous results. And if we cease praying to and thanking God, we dry up spiritually.

When we pray on a continual basis, gratefully inviting God into our everyday lives, sharing our joys and needs, our anxiety level drops. And we no longer feel compelled to cope in negative ways. Talking with God nourishes our soul and helps us face life's daily surprises.

*Lord, thank You for the privilege of talking
to You. Teach me to practice Your presence so that
I can pray "without ceasing."*

Make It Personal: When, where and how will you fit prayer into your life today (if you're reading this in the morning) or tomorrow (if you're reading this at night)?

Released to Enjoy

*Lord, it is good for us to be here. If you wish,
I will put up three shelters.*

Matthew 17:4

"Jesus, this is incredible!" said Peter. "I'd really love to commemorate it by building three memorials. What do you say?" Jesus had invited Peter, James and John into the mountains, where they saw Jesus' face shine like never before and His clothes turn pure white. Then two Old Testament heroes, Elijah and Moses, appeared in conversation with the radiant Jesus.

Peter valued this extraordinary moment; still, he wanted to do *more*. Like Peter, we can sometimes try too hard to augment God's blessings and prolong our spiritual high. We want to sustain the sense of awe and intimacy that we seek and sometimes experience with our Savior and other Christians. Consequently, we may work ourselves into spiritual overload by saying yes to more meetings, studies and service. When that doesn't work as we hope, we increase the intensity or give up, disillusioned by it all.

Yet God wants to release us from both approaches. We're invited to join the Father, Son and Spirit on the mountain top or in the valley. It is as if Jesus says, "Come with Me. I'll show you who I am and share My glory with you. You'll see. Stay, watch, marvel and enjoy."

*Lord Jesus, here I am. Here You are.
I want to stop trying so hard to perfect our
relationship and just be in Your presence.*

Make It Personal: Sometime during this week, take a walk (or do another reflective activity) and just *be* with God. Jot down what happens and your feelings about it.

In Love with Me?

I have loved you with an everlasting love.

Jeremiah 31:3

While recovering from burnout, I enjoyed a few days away. Eating breakfast alone, I listened to some background music. To the strumming of a peaceful guitar, a soloist sang, "God is in love with His people. God is in love with me."

Tears filled my eyes and splashed on my cheeks. For a woman who doesn't cry much, this surprised me. "What a liberating idea, Lord." I smile now, remembering that moment when my soul—empty for so long—filled with fresh hope. I also recall my next thought, which threatened my newfound contentment: "But is this true that You're in love with me, Lord?"

When I returned to my room, I searched my Bible and concordance for affirmation. Then I read, "The Lord appeared . . . saying, 'I have loved you with an everlasting love'" (Jeremiah 31:3).[67]

"It *is* true," I whispered. "God is in love with me." That day I wrote in my journal, *Lord, I'm amazed that I needn't perform to draw You near. Neither must I strive to win Your approval. You smile at me as a lover who is completely enamored with his mate. My heart catches a moment of pure joy as I contemplate this truth—for time and eternity, I am loved by You.*

*Lord, help me continue to believe
that You're in love with me even when my
mind and emotions insist otherwise.*

Make It Personal: You might write this verse, Jeremiah 31:3, on a small card and put it on your desk or car visor to remind you daily of God's constant love.

God Isn't Like That

A bruised reed he will not break.

Isaiah 42:3

"What a day! Everything went wrong!" moans my friend. "Our car broke down and it cost $800 to have it repaired this morning. When I got home, the washer had overflowed and flooded the kitchen. Then the school nurse called to say my son has chicken pox!

"I wonder if God's punishing me," her voice breaks as she continues. "Maybe He thinks we don't give enough time or money to our church. I should do more."

Yet, I remind her, a seven-year-old car that breaks down, a child who contracts chicken pox and a washer that malfunctions and overflows merely reveal the inevitable consequences of living in an imperfect world. These things just happen—sometimes they're spread over several months; other times they happen in one day!

As Danielle and I chat, she acknowledges that sometimes she views her heavenly Father through the memories of an earthly father who sent her to bed without dinner for accidentally spilling her milk—or even mispronouncing a word. "I *know* God isn't like that," she says. "That Bible verse we read today really helps: *a bruised reed He will not break.* Please keep reminding me of that."

God doesn't mistreat His children. When we hurt financially, emotionally, physically or spiritually, He cares. He sent His Son to prove just how much.

Lord, how comforting to know that You won't
crush me when I'm weak and needy.

Make It Personal: In *THE MESSAGE,* Eugene Peterson paraphrases Isaiah 42:3 this way: "He won't brush aside the bruised and the hurt." When have you felt like a "bruised reed"?

Makes Me Smile

"O Jerusalem, Jerusalem . . . how often I have longed to
gather your children together, as a hen gathers her chicks
under his wings, but you were not willing."

Matthew 23:37

Do you want a glimpse into the heart of the Son of God? He said, "So often I yearn to surround you with My love and protection, like a mother hen shields her chicks from danger under her wings, but you won't let Me. You just push Me away."

Jesus, God's Son, was talking to the educated, religious people who lived near Him. They saw Him heal, witnessed all the good He did. They heard God's message of reconciliation. But they didn't like what they heard, because performing just right for God was their religion. So they refused God's invitation of freedom, intimacy and mercy. It broke Jesus' heart.

Although I genuinely desire God's help, still I think I push Him aside sometimes. I don't want to. Yet I fear what will happen if I quit trying so hard to serve. Surrender feels so risky, so vulnerable—and messy. I'm afraid I'll do it wrong.

"Of course you will make mistakes; everybody makes mistakes, but you will begin to better recognize my voice as we continue to grow our relationship," says the voice of God's Spirit in the bestselling book *The Shack* by William P. Young.[68] God longs to free me from fear and draw me close. You, too. *Really.*

Lord, for today I stop running away.
I'll probably flub up. But I don't think You'll mind.
And that makes me smile.

Make It Personal: How do you picture Jesus' protective love?

Generous Resources

To him who is able to do immeasurably more
than all we ask or imagine, according to his power
that is at work within us.

Ephesians 3:20

A recent article in our newspaper included these instructions: *Preserve resources by using less energy. Reduce, Reuse, and Recycle. Conserve water.* Many ecologists warn that we are systematically depleting our natural resources. If we don't conserve, they say, we won't have enough to survive on this planet. Although some don't agree with these predictions, others remain genuinely anxious about our future environmental supplies. The advice? *We need to be careful by reducing our consumption.*

Several years ago, I experienced a similar uneasy feeling spiritually. I didn't want to be selfish or greedy. I wondered whether I'd already presumed on God's goodness and generosity long enough, perhaps using up my designated portion of His available resources. When that happened, I noticed that I began to pre-judge and ration out my prayer requests.

Then God, true to His bountiful personality and loving-kindness, assured me: "Joan, don't worry. I'm willing and able to do and give far beyond what you can dream or plan."

You and I can ask God to save, help, guide, intercede, comfort, heal, forgive, direct, sustain and protect us, our families, friends, neighbors, pastors, missionaries, local and national governments and the world. We needn't be concerned about conserving our prayers. His power cannot be depleted. God has unlimited resources.

Lord, Your wealth knows no boundaries.
You can do far above what I can ask
or imagine in my entire lifetime.

Make It Personal: Name several ways God has been generous with you.

On the Receiving End

Your faith will help me,
and my faith will help you.

Romans 1:12, *NCV*

"I'll be praying as you recover from your dental surgery," I promised my friend as she left our Bible study and headed for the clinic. I figured the operation would upset this working mother's schedule and energy level for the next few days.

"Oh, don't bother taking time to pray for me," she said with a flip of her wrist. "I'll be okay."

Although her response was a little extreme, it touched a raw nerve in my soul. Some of us believe that it's godly to give, but we balk at asking. It feels uncomfortable being on the receiving end. I admit that I have a little trouble with this. I don't wish to be self-centered or disturb others with my concerns, because everyone's to-do list is already so long.

Yet understanding how to give *and* take is part of growing spiritually. We actually give others joy and strengthen their faith when we ask for and then gratefully accept their help. Paul realized that he could learn significantly from the people he loved and ministered to in the name of Christ. He didn't insist on doing all the giving. He longed to visit them and receive help, as well as provide it.

Lord, help me relax and allow
others to give and nurture me as
I care and support them.

Make It Personal: What family, work or personal concern are you facing this week? Ask at least one caring friend to support you in prayer for this specific issue.

Reflecting God's Nature

So God created man in his own image,
in the image of God he created him.

Genesis 1:27

"Sometimes I feel lonely," revealed the mother of three preschoolers and wife of a busy executive. "I wish my husband would more spend time with the children and me. But I guess I'm being selfish. I shouldn't let my wants or needs get the best of me. God probably wants to teach me to be strong and forget about my personal desires."

Over the years I've heard many similar comments.

Our longings for intimacy aren't wrong. God made us with a basic need to be nurtured and loved. In *Mending the Soul*, Steven R. Tracy writes, "By virtue of being made in God's image, humans have the capacity, longing, and need for intimate relationship based on the truth that God himself is a relational God who is in intimate relationship within his own divine being."[69] Although admittedly difficult to fully understand the triune nature of God, the fact remains that the Father, Son and Spirit work together intimately, and we reflect their nature.

God isn't surprised by the intensity of our natural relational desires. They are part of being human, as well as part of being made in the image of God. God delights in our desires for intimacy. We need not scold ourselves for what God accepts.

Lord God, in love You created me.
You know my legitimate heart's desires, and You
don't tell me they're wrong. Thank You for treating me
with such acceptance and loving-kindness.

Make It Personal: In what area of your life are you being too hard on yourself? Go ahead. You can answer that. It's okay.

Spiritual Calisthenics

Who could ever offer to the Lord
enough to induce him to act?

Romans 11:35, *TLB*

"I should have had a longer quiet time this morning. My day would have gone better."

We may not admit it at first, yet it appears that some of us, like the busy young woman who uttered these words, believe that we can pray, study, read or serve enough to induce God to bless us and grant us trouble-free days. However, God won't be manipulated—and that's a good thing! His loving involvement in our lives doesn't fluctuate in proportion to how many minutes we put into our quiet time each day—or how we grade its quality or our spirituality.

"His love cannot be bought with our faithfulness, because it has already been purchased by His death on the cross!" writes Vonda Skelton in her book *Seeing Through the Lies*.[70] We've been reunited with God the Father through Jesus' grace-filled sacrifice. When we spend quiet time in His presence, we gain much, but that doesn't alter the reality of His consistent mercy, faithfulness and care. We can learn to relax and enjoy God's company without trying to keep score on ourselves. As His children, God acts on our behalf regardless of how many spiritual calisthenics we perform.

Lord, I want to spend time with You. I long to know
You and understand Your words. You are God. I know
I could never do enough to make You love me more.
In this reality, I feel secure and blessed.

Make It Personal: When have you tried too hard to make it just right in your quiet times with the Lord? What was the result?

God's Surprises

*Then the angel of God, who had been traveling in front of
Israel's army, withdrew and went behind them. The pillar
of cloud also moved from in front and stood behind them,
coming between the armies of Egypt and Israel.*

Exodus 14:19-20

With the Egyptians hot on the heels of the liberated Israelite people, God changed His protective tactics. For days, God's angel had effectively led them from the front of the ranks. But now God moved the angel to the rear. As a result, the approaching Egyptians couldn't see the Israelites and Moses guided the people safely across the Red Sea.

God altered the way He had worked previously.

Sometimes we put God in a box, making declarations like, "God healed me *this* way; He'll do it the same way for you" or "Here's how He helped me choose a partner; just wait—God will work this way for you, too" or "Here's the Bible study plan I use; you should, too."

Yet God doesn't use a cookie-cutter method to produce His will in people's lives. He has all the diverse resources in the universe at His command. Even though He may have never moved in a specific way before, we need not panic; God knows what each individual needs to grow and mature.

*Lord, sometimes You work as You have before;
other times, You surprise me. I don't have every answer,
so I'll step aside. Do Your job in Your way.*

Make It Personal: Name a time God surprised you by the different approach He used to bring about good results in someone else's life. What about in your life?

Tomorrow's Overconfidence

But he replied, "Lord, I am ready to go
with you to prison and to death."

Luke 22:33

"Don't worry, Lord," said Peter. "I'll stand by You. I'm ready to go to jail for You. I'd even die for You."

"Peter, this very day, you'll pretend you don't even know Me," Jesus replied.

Peter could have responded, "Oh, my! Lord, if that's the case, please help me. I don't want to act that way. I need courage to meet the coming challenges." But instead he said, "There may be trouble ahead, but I can handle it. I'll never stop trusting You, Lord. Whatever happens, I know my faith will see me through."

Like Peter, I sometimes bite off huge chunks of faith at a time. "Lord, there'll never come a time when I won't completely trust You," I promise. But then my overconfidence becomes more than I can handle. Ruminating over next week's deadlines, tasks, potential problems and victories, as well as my loved ones' dilemmas and possible solutions, all while trying to remind myself that God is in charge and it will all be okay, can give me spiritual indigestion.

So I'm learning that I don't need to guarantee the future. Instead, I can live each day by faith. Faith is a gift from God and I gratefully accept it one moment, one task, one dilemma at a time.

Lord, release me from the burden of tomorrow's faith.
It's too heavy for me. I'll trust You for my "now"
and leave the "forever" with You.

Make It Personal: When does "forever faith" feel too big for you? What problem or personal concern will you commit to God "just for today" that might prove overwhelming if you had to guarantee that commitment for an entire lifetime?

Into the Silence

Be still before the Lord and
wait patiently for him.

Psalm 37:7

While on a getaway designed for rest and recuperation after a hectic few months, I heard an inner voice chiding (now I realize that it was my Mr. Should Bully): *Don't just sit there. Do something. Pray. Write in your journal. Read the Bible.* Instead, I ignored the interior slave driver. I sat alone with my thoughts and God for several hours. That was new behavior for me.

Just today, a coaching client reported about her recent vacation: Determined to leave her mounting tasks behind, she didn't load her carry-on with files, books and work. Even her husband noticed her lighter luggage. However, when she got to the motel room, she noticed that she hadn't packed her Bible, either. *That's not good,* she thought. The next morning, when normally she would jump up to read her Bible and launch into the "I'm a Bible teacher, show me something new, Lord" mode, instead she spent her minutes waiting, chatting and listening to the Lord. "It *was* good," she admitted.

Although we may choose to spend organized time studying, journaling and praying, we needn't do so in order for God to love and speak with us. We can relax, be still and wait. Even when the insight or inspiration doesn't flow freely, God is there. He invites you and me into the silence with Him.

> *Lord, I love knowing about You. But I want*
> *to spend time with You, too. I'm not*
> *always sure how. Please guide me.*

Make It Personal: What do you suppose God is up to in the "silence"? Why not ask Him?

Out with Bogus Rules

We have a great High Priest who has gone to heaven, Jesus the
Son of God. . . . [He] understands our weaknesses, for he faced all
of the same temptations we do, yet he did not sin. So let us come
boldly to the throne of our gracious God. There we will receive his
mercy, and we will find grace to help us when we need it.

Hebrews 4:14-16, *NLT*

"What if I say it wrong?" she mumbled. "What'll I do if he misunder-
stands?" This young working wife and mother planned to tell her husband that she felt sad, overworked and exhausted. She wanted to ask
him for help, but she was obsessed with doing it right.

Some of us may be like this young woman when we prepare to talk
with God. We worry about saying the right words, at the right place, in
the right way. We try to fit our prayers into a rigidly calculated formula.

God is not overly concerned with our exact words, specific posture
or perfect methods. He accepts us with open arms as we come in genuine faith. We can speak freely to God through Jesus, even when we
don't have it all figured out. He cares how we feel, how confused we are
and what we think at the moment. God listens patiently and then guides
us through our needy times.

Lord, I'm throwing out the bogus
rules I've had about You. This new way of
approaching You is going to take some practice.
Thanks for being patient with me.

Make It Personal: Underline the words from today's Scripture passage
that help you feel close to God.

Frenzied Prayer

The effectual fervent prayer of a
righteous man availeth much.

James 5:16, *KJV*

After I memorized James 5:16, it quickly became one of my favorite Bible verses. I longed to become a woman of prayer, one whose prayers "availed much." I got to know God better as my prayer life expanded, even though I didn't always know how to do it perfectly!

And then I began to associate the word "fervent" with intensity, urgency and forcefulness. I thought my prayers might get more results if my heart was tied in a knot. Although not noticeably pushy or boisterous, internally I felt driven to prove to myself and to God how much I cared. Maybe I thought that if I were passionate enough, God would decide to act on my behalf.

As I became less obsessed in other areas of my life, a relaxed and trusting attitude spilled over into my prayer life. Oh, I still cry, laugh, question and interact excitedly with God in prayer. But I've discovered that it is not my overwrought or inflamed words that move the hand of God. Creativity, energy and enthusiasm flow from Him, but obsession and drivenness do not. I don't know quite how to convey this, but here's what I now believe this verse means: The active, energetic, bold prayer of a person who has decided to believe Jesus and live within God's expansive boundaries is powerful and effective.

Lord, teach me the difference between fervent
and frenzied prayer. I calmly believe that You
will accomplish what I cannot.

Make It Personal: What do you think is the difference between fervent and frenzied prayer? Either way, just pray today.

Nourishing Your Soul

*Your own soul is nourished when you are kind;
it is destroyed when you are cruel.*

Proverbs 11:17, *TLB*

I sat in a lovely old library surrounded by the written wisdom of well-known Bible scholars. Pulling a book from the shelf, I settled into an over-stuffed chair to read. Sounds pretty good, huh? But these words glared at me from the page: "Christians may burn out, but they must not rust out."[71] The author probably meant that it's better to act than not, yet I winced because this statement used to be my unspoken creed. Practicing it caused me to become a walking dead person. What good was I to anyone then?

Adhering to this philosophy (which as a teenager I adopted from my mentors), I assisted, befriended, encouraged and nurtured others, yet neglected myself. In his book *Burnout*, Myron Rush explains, "When you burn both ends of a candle, it may produce twice as much light, but the candle burns out twice as fast. People . . . discover that all of their mental, emotional and physical energies have been consumed."[72]

You and I are part of God's creation, just like the people we serve. Our souls are nourished when treated with kindness, and they're destroyed when we're cruel to ourselves. We respond to life with less anxiety and greater joy when we're considerate not only of others, but of ourselves, as well.

*Kind Father, Your grace has touched my malnourished soul
and brought back hope. Help me stop mistreating myself
so that I can thrive to serve others and You.*

Make It Personal: Choose one way to nourish yourself this week.

Quit Thrashing Inside

*Cease striving and know
that I am God.*

Psalm 46:10, *NASB*

"The harder I try to follow all the instructions in the many books I read about being a servant and better Christian, the more I run myself down. After attending too many Bible studies and striving too hard to pray and serve, I ended up numb. I don't like feeling numb. I just want to relax with God and listen to His voice calming me down," revealed my friend Becky.

Another friend, Mary Jane, shared her spiritual over-doing story, as well: "My spiritual walk has focused on trying to be a good Christian woman, doing what I should and avoiding what I should not. I love to study, but it became exhausting. I now know it's not about the 'must dos' and I feel transforming freedom in just *being* with Christ."

Sometimes our striving to know more *about* God means that we keep so busy studying and reading that we unintentionally neglect experiencing God Himself—and it wears us out. The psalmist wrote, "Be still, and know that I am God." What an encouragement to quit thrashing inside and to hush and relax in who God is.

*Lord, sometimes I'm in such a race inside
that even the thought of slowing down to relax with You
is confusing. How can I expect to prove my competence if I
cease striving? Oh, God, I need Your help.*

Make It Personal: How do you identify with Becky and Mary Jane? What spiritual to-do will you delete from your list this month? (*Psst.* This deletion is not for *forever*, so relax!)

A Beautiful Thing

> While Jesus was in Bethany in the home of a man known
> as Simon the Leper, a woman came to him with an alabaster jar
> of very expensive perfume, which she poured on his head as he
> was reclining at the table. When the disciples saw this, they were
> indignant. . . . Aware of this, Jesus said . . . "Why are you bothering
> this woman? She has done a beautiful thing to me."
>
> Matthew 26:6-8,10

When this woman worshiped the Lord in her unique way, she risked the disapproval of the important men who surrounded Jesus. And indeed, the men's immediate reactions proved to be condemning and critical. Yet Jesus' response splashed acceptance, validation and honor on her—and on all who would likewise honor her praise-filled act.

Sometimes I'm intent on worshiping, praising and serving God in just the *right* way, perhaps because I've felt the sting of disapproval when I haven't done "it" like others might. However, Jesus' response to this woman's act of love encourages me to relax and be myself in my relationship with Him, regardless of another's reactions.

Likewise, I want to learn to accept my fellow Christians in their genuine expression of heartfelt worship and service. There are no wasted resources when you and I praise the triune God. Worshiping perfectly is not important to Him. God views my authentic praise and adoration as a "beautiful thing." And yours, too!

> *Lord, help me express my thoughts*
> *and praise without embarrassment,*
> *and allow others to do the same.*

Make It Personal: How do you desire to worship God? How does that differ from your mate's or best friend's preference? What is God showing you about these differences?

Prayer Without Strings

Since we have confidence to enter the Most Holy Place
by the blood of Jesus. . . . Let us draw near to God with a
sincere heart in full assurance of faith.

Hebrews 10:19,22

As I learn to be less indispensable to others, I find my prayer life changing. The more I realize that I don't have all the answers, the less compelled I feel to tell God exactly how to work.

In *My Utmost for His Highest*, Oswald Chambers writes, "Beware of imagining that intercession means bringing our personal sympathies into the presence of God and demanding that He does what we ask."[73] Perhaps the fulfillment of requests such as, "Lord, make my daughter choose the college I attended" or "Remove Sue's hurt" could detour God's plan for the daughter and for Sue. What if God plans for the young woman to attend another college so that she can meet her future husband there? Or what if God, even though He didn't order the hurt, is preparing to transform Sue through her difficult experiences?

When we believe we're responsible for our loved one's wellbeing and happiness, we may spend our prayer time dictating to God on their behalf. It's really exhausting, because it's not our job.

Only Jesus is Savior and Redeemer. Because of His death and resurrection, we can come before a Holy God with total confidence and share our concerns without demanding the answer we think is best. We then have the exciting privilege of watching God work.

Lord, with no strings attached,
I ask You to work powerfully in my life
and my loved ones' lives.

Make It Personal: What is God showing you about intercessory prayer?

Enjoying God

The LORD your God is with you, he is mighty to save.
He will take great delight in you, he will quiet you with his love,
he will rejoice over you with singing.

Zephaniah 3:17

"Each bed-time, I would beat myself up for not spending enough time
with God, for failing to accomplish more for Him, for not being a perfect Christian mom," said my friend Suzanne. "I thought this nightly
scolding ritual would help me grow spiritually, but instead I became
more dissatisfied, inflexible and tired. Then, as I studied the Minor
Prophets[74] and read Zephaniah 3:17, I sensed God accepting me instead
of condemning me. It was my turning point."

I think God longs for us to *want* to be with Him so much that we become creative with our desire. For example, Suzanne shared that she recently purchased a decorative metal cross at a garden store and placed it
at the entrance to her long driveway. This reminded her to drop her frustration and resentment at Christ's cross so that she could face her less-
than-perfect daily circumstances with a freer heart.

And just this morning on my walk, with eyes wide open, I praised
God through the alphabet: *Lord, you're Awesome, Beautiful, Creator... Forgiving, Gracious... Joy-giver*—and on through Z. (*X* represented "Extraordinary," *Z* stood for "the Beginning and the *End*." I told you it's a
creative adventure!)

Our individual relationships with the triune God (Father, Son and
Spirit) deepen when we move past our religious routines and enjoy
Him expansively.

Lord, Your love liberates me.

Make It Personal: In what creative way will you enjoy God's company
this week?[75]

Breathing Room for Your Soul

Remember my biofeedback fiasco at the physical therapist's office? The P.T. wanted to teach me to breathe more deeply, but I didn't *get* it. I wasn't trying to be rebellious; I really *believed* that performing relaxation techniques was unspiritual. Forced to oppose that belief, my brain released negative impulses and my muscles tightened.

Experts reveal that most of us take for granted the 20,000 breaths God gives us each day.[76] The first time I practiced deep breathing methods repeatedly and intentionally, I was stuck in traffic, fretting that I'd never make my appointment on time. So I tried the approach the P.T. had taught me. After breathing slowly and deeply for several minutes, the unimaginable happened: My defeated "Not again. Oh, well," became a genuinely smile-able "So what? Being tardy isn't the end of the world." I arrived late, but not frazzled.

It happened again this evening. Before our daughter has her baby (any day now!) I want to meet a deadline. Do you feel the pressure, too? Maybe you're trying to complete a résumé on time, to get your son to college, to wrap up your wedding prep or to finish that school project due tomorrow. Of course, you want to do it just right and the last thing you feel you need is to take time for a breather. Yet tonight, I did—and my soul, mind and body calmed.

In our over-scheduled, over-worried, over-whatevered lives, it's difficult to apply the patience required to process personal change.[77] Yesterday a coaching partner moaned, "I should be 'fixed' by now. Yet I still struggle. A mentor told me that God usually heals instantly. Not happening here. I'm confused." Together, we brainstormed examples of how God approves of *process*: A seed grows over time into a healthy tree or bush that produces flowers, fruit or vegetables. Creation took several swoops of God's hand. Jesus navigated childhood and adolescence to finally fulfill His purpose at age 33. Prospective mommies wait nine months for their babies to arrive. Those babies learn to walk, talk, reason and work after months and years of trial and error—it's never instantaneous. Indeed, God sanctions and smiles at the *process* of growth and transformation.

Growth for me is an unpredictable adventure. I know it sounds odd, but I've ceased crawling internally. In my mental image, I didn't have room to stand, because I moved through a small tunnel. Ironically, I visualized myself thriving and advancing on my knees, as if that was the only way spiritual progress could be made. Discussing this with my life coach, I decided that I didn't wish to crawl anymore.[78] The imaginary walls expanded and I stood. My breathing is freer (it's easier when I'm not bent over!). Standing up means that I accept how good it is to say no at times and that I stop doing for others what they can do for themselves, allowing them to implement their own ideas and dreams. I think my narrow tunnel had been built with the *shoulds* and *musts* I've heard and internalized. I don't like to admit it, but I probably allowed others' opinions to keep me on my knees. Yet, I don't have to crawl; I have colorful options that are beyond mere black-and-white thinking.

Jesus' words "Be perfect" (Matthew 5:48) and "Be merciful" (Luke 6:36-37) aren't do-it-right-or-else edicts from an unreasonable leader, but loving guidelines encouraging me to grow from the inside out and to experience respite from trying too hard to appear godly. It's a grace-filled, gratitude-creating heart thing.

Perhaps you, like me, have at times believed something (or someone) is either "fantastic and perfect" or "messed up and toss-worthy." *The truth?* In this world, imperfection and excellence (or good-enough) coexist. Our work, families, emotions, bodies, churches, plans and faith don't have to be perfect to be wonderful. God alone is perfect, and He sends me gratitude-laced "grace drops," followed by sunbeams of relief. I agree with the psalmist; He is "breathing room for my soul" (see Psalm 62:1-2, *THE MESSAGE*).

Good Enough!

Everything is so weary and tiresome! No matter how
much we see, we are never satisfied.

Ecclesiastes 1:8, *NLT*

I drove up to the motel entrance, turned off the engine and walked into the lobby. Glancing around, I concluded, *This place won't do. I'll find another one.* So I climbed back into the van to scout out the city's other motels. No vacancy at the next one, but I didn't like the atmosphere anyway.

At the third motel, I walked the hallways, examined the cafe and pool area, and was nearly ready to retreat to the van to continue my hunt, when I stopped. "Hey, Joan, when will anything be adequate?" I whispered. "You don't know if you'll find something better around the corner. So just cool it. This motel is good enough." I unloaded the van and stayed the night.

Over the years of working with women—me included!—I've noticed that we're frequently on edge, anxious that our decisions, judgments and actions be just right. We can get overly concerned that our house, children, relationships, jobs, vacations, exercise, volunteer time and church involvements appear fault-free. We really yearn to be fair, committed, knowledgeable and wise. And that's commendable. It really is. Yet we get tired of trying so hard, of not quite being satisfied.

By accepting our imperfect reality as good enough, we're free to enjoy the moment, have fun with others, feel our gratitude and relax inside. Truly, breath-filled relief.

Lord, I'm "good enough" because of Your grace.
Today I'll let go of trying to make everything
around and inside me just right.

Make It Personal: Say "So what?" 10 times today!

Adventure of Faith

I will repay you for the years the locusts have eaten. . . .
You will have plenty to eat, until you are full, you will praise . . .
your God, who has worked wonders for you.

Joel 2:25-26

I've struggled and worked so hard. I'm disappointed in my relationships. I haven't been true to myself or become the person God called me to be. My mind is fried. My body hurts. And I'm angry. I wonder if I'll ever be whole and happy again. I wrote these words when I finally admitted that I couldn't "gut it out" anymore and that I needed help.

I experienced chronic pain as a result of my over-doing, over-caring, over-achieving and over-spiritualizing. I figured that if I just tried a little harder, everything would have to get better. But it didn't work. Disappointment took over, my dreams eaten up.

Perhaps you identify, whether completely or only a little, in one specific slice of your life. It hurts, and you wonder if that part of you will ever be lush again.

God promises those of us who choose to believe Him that He will repay us for the hurtful times. I couldn't fathom how He would accomplish it for me, and I don't presume to know how He will do it for you. Yet trusting God is definitely an adventure worthy of our faith.

*Lord, even as I realize that my life will never
be perfectly perfect on this earth, I believe that You
can work wonders in my disappointment and
repay me for the destructive times.
I'm a little afraid, but I want to trust You.*

Make It Personal: How have you been trying to "gut it out"?

The Diversion Game

Going through the motions doesn't please you, a flawless
performance is nothing to you. I learned God-worship when
my pride was shattered. Heart-shattered lives ready for love
don't for a moment escape God's notice.

Psalm 51:17, *THE MESSAGE*

"How can I help you?" I asked.

"I want a gift for my five-year-old daughter. She's in the hospital."
His companion moved to look at the merchandise behind me.

"How about this cute shirt?" I asked.

"Hm-mmm. Maybe I should check with her mother. Would you
please hold this shirt while I make a phone call?" He glanced at his
friend who joined him by the door. "We'll be right back," they promised.

When I walked back to the counter, I found the cash register open
and empty. We'd been robbed! The noble gift-buying story had diverted
my attention from the real issue: a theft was under way.

Sometimes my noble attempts at making life just right divert attention from the urgent matters of my heart. Perhaps you've noticed this
in your life, too. No matter what we've been told, God cares more about
the inner you and me than how we look or what we do. God *will* give us
insight, as we ask Him to. Then, with His help, we can grow from the
inside out, adopting authentic relationships with ourselves, others and
God Himself.

Lord, I don't want to divert attention away
from the truly meaningful things in life.
So here I am—imperfect and needy. Hold me close
and show me how to live authentically.

Make It Personal: What diverts your attention and sabotages your re-
solve to grow?

Little by Little

The unfolding of your words gives light;
it gives understanding to the simple.

Psalm 119:130

R-r-r-ling! R-r-r-ling! We lunged toward the phone. Grandma Joan (that's me!) got there first.

"Your seventh grandchild, Calissa Jolie, is here!" exclaimed my son-in-law, Adam. In the background I heard Calissa's three sisters cheer.

Papa and I enjoy taking our three grandsons and four granddaughters on adventures and watching them learn about life, others, themselves and God. Yet in our exuberance, we don't force 1-week-old Calissa to stand alone, or 22-month-old Sam to recite the pastor's Bible text or 9-year-old Annika to drive us to the store. We don't expect 8-year-old Max to pitch for the Arizona Diamondbacks or kindergartner Luke to graduate from high school next year. Neither would we throw 4-year-old Lesia into a lake and yell, "Swim across, kid!" And even though 5-year-old Kirsten builds great Tinkertoy houses, we'd never insist she renovate our guest room. Obviously, these expectations would all be extremely unreasonable.

Likewise, our heavenly Father—who delights in watching us develop, too—doesn't push us beyond our capabilities and understanding. He waits until we're ready. If God told us everything about ourselves, the world and life all at once, we'd be overwhelmed and crushed. Instead, He encourages us based on our spiritual, mental and emotional age-level. God's gentle unfolding plan increases our insight and encourages our consistent growth.

Father, thanks for nurturing my development
little by little. Help me to be as patient as You are with
my imperfect attempts at maturity.

Make It Personal: List the ways you've grown during the last few months. Plan a simple celebration. What sounds fun to you?

Daily Gift

This is the day the Lord has made,
let us rejoice and be glad in it.

Psalm 118:24

The other day after doing research, I met with a client, which earned me enough money to pay a small bill. I called my agent and followed up on several speaking leads. After creating and printing some brochures, I picked up a prescription and dropped by the grocery store. While working on this book, I washed some laundry, stopping to make a quick dinner. I called my dad long-distance, pressed Richard's suit for his trip tomorrow and went to bed ruminating about how I could meet upcoming deadlines.

On a different day, after writing for a few hours early in the morning, I took a walk and noticed the seasonal pink blossoms on the cactus next door. I drove the golf cart to the pool area, sat by the waterfall and sang quietly. (Nobody was around!) I wrote in my journal and met a friend for coffee (I had a chai tea). After a simple dinner, I sat and watched the sunset over the distant mountains and then played a few favorite hymns on the piano.

As I thought about both days, I wondered, "Which one was more valuable?" Lately, most days have been nonstop working ones. Another "day off" like the one I wrote about sounds welcome. But I realize my life doesn't consist solely of one kind of day. No matter what a day brings, it is a gift from God—and a reason to celebrate.

Lord, You made this day and gave
it to me to enjoy. Thank You.

Make It Personal: Describe your yesterday and your last "day off."

A Smile-able Truth!

"What good is it for a man to gain the whole world,
and yet lose or forfeit his very self?"

Luke 9:25

Hard work never hurt anybody!

Perhaps you, too, have heard this adage. It's true that balanced, faithful work is beneficial, fueling self-respect, personal responsibility and genuine interdependence. Still, when we push too far, hard work is not good for us.

The Japanese have a name for it: *karoshi*, meaning "death by overwork." Striving to be the most productive nation, individual Japanese forfeit family time, spiritual enrichment *and* their lives. Years ago, when I first heard about *karoshi*, reports indicated the death toll at 10,000 per year for individuals driven by corporate management to routinely work overtime, take little or no vacation, ignore physical signs of stress, and never complain. I didn't hear much more until this week, when I read an article in *The Arizona Republic* titled " 'Overwork' Killed Engineer."[79] A Japanese labor bureau ruled that one of Toyota's top car engineers, age 45, died from working too many hours. His family was allowed to collect insurance benefits. I assume that they would rather still have him around.

God offers us respite from our work—whether at home, at church or on the job—compassionate understanding for our hurts, grace from over-trying, and power in our humanness. So we can stop heeding our internal or external slave drivers.

Now that's a smile-able truth.

Lord, I'm beginning to get it. You're not the one
pushing me to try so hard to do it all just right. Sometimes I'm
slow in understanding this, so please remind me often.

Make It Personal: What does your over-trying or over-doing cost you?

Refreshed Each Dawn

I remember my affliction and my wandering,
the bitterness and the gall. . . . Yet this I call to mind and
therefore I have hope: Because of the Lord's great love we are
not consumed, for his compassions never fail. They are new
every morning; great is your faithfulness.

Lamentations 3:19-22

In a reflective mood one morning, I jotted these words on a piece of scrap paper:

I am an open, bleeding wound that's not allowed to heal. I feel like I have a broken leg, but I just keep walking on it. (The only difference is that it's my mind and soul that are broken!) I'm standing on the outside of life watching myself go through the motions, but I want to participate again. I want to feel like a real person, to be whole once more. God, I want to know and feel Your love. I long for my performing and doing to become one with who I am. I know that it can be.

That last sentence astonishes me. It reveals that I hadn't entirely lost hope, even though I felt sad, disappointed and resentful. One day at a time, God's love reached out to me. He bandaged my wounds and set my broken heart. It took time, but I'm participating in life again— and have been for years. Every dawn, whether it is sunny or cloudy, God renews me. He wants to do the same for you. Please let God's love refresh you.

Lord, I don't know just how You will do it,
but I'm hopeful. I want to live.

Make It Personal: Make a list of what you're grateful for today.

Facing
Frustration

Your throne, O LORD, has been established from time immemorial. . . .
Mightier than the violent raging of the seas, mightier than the breakers
on the shore—the LORD above is mightier than these!

Psalm 93:2,4

"I got frustrated while working in New Orleans recently. On a previous
trip, I helped prepare houses for refurbishing. Now it appeared my hard
work—and that of others—became lunch for a bulldozer. So I grabbed
my Bible, looking for comfort, and found Psalm 93:2-4: 'In the midst of
this, I AM,' assures God. Although disappointed, I found peace knowing
that God, who is bigger than any hurricane, still reigns on His throne
in the middle of apparent unfairness. Later I learned that people were
actually living in homes that we had cleared in another area. Not everything met face to face with a bulldozer!"

This email from a journalist friend reminded me of what must have
been a frustrating experience for Jesus. He carefully prepared, prayed
and chose His team (see Luke 6:12-16). He planned to equip them to
take over His ministry. Still, Judas, one of those men, betrayed Him.

Although we care deeply, work hard, pray and prepare, our lives don't
always look perfect or feel great. Our meticulously organized plans may
not come to fruition as we expect. At times, people let us down. Jesus understands our frustration. He reigns with His Father in the midst of our
questions and offers us the assurance of His powerful presence.

Lord Jesus, thanks for Your comfort
and understanding.

Make It Personal: Name a frustrating time in your life when God assured you of His mighty presence. How does this help you today?

Management Contract with God

Commit your way to the LORD,
trust also in Him, and He will do it.

Psalm 37:5, *NASB*

"Sorry I'm late," my young employee said as she headed toward the time clock. "Transmission fell out of my car!" she yelled over her shoulder. "Mom's gambling again. I had another fight with my boyfriend. Neither one would bring me to work. I can't afford to fix my car 'cause my credit cards are maxed out again. I don't know what to do." She whirled around and blurted, "I wish God would just give me a break."

Perhaps if you and I were completely honest, we'd admit to having a similar thought on occasion. (Not often, you know. Just when we get "out of sorts" with life! Right?) However, our loving God doesn't walk into our lives and change everything just because we grumble.

Once we partner with God, He becomes our personal manager—the wisest and most caring manager we could ever have. Working for our ultimate good, He counsels us how to heal past damage, overcome self-defeating habits and experience contentment as we trust Him for the future. You and I benefit when we accept life on our Creator's terms.

*Lord, I've decided to trust You with my life
and circumstances. As you know, things are a little
messy right now. Please be my life manager.
I believe You have my best interests in mind and that
partnering with You is the way to go.*

Make It Personal: Consider writing a one- to three-sentence management contract with God. Sign it and date it. Then put a copy in your wallet or where you can find it easily.

Do It Scared!

Whenever I am afraid, I will trust in you.

Psalm 56:3

"Wait 'til you see the big elk," said the caretaker. "With *huge* racks. They usually show up at night. Probably so we can't get a photo!"

Several days later, on the dirt road leading from the cabin into town, I saw them—bounding toward me. Glad I was in the car! The word *big* doesn't describe these elk. I gawked as they galloped past. To my surprise, the first two elk suddenly stopped at the fence, gently lifted their front legs and hopped over. But when the third one jolted to a stop, he paused, walking up and down the fence line. Then I noticed he had only half a rack—where one side of antlers should have been was merely a stub. *What fight did he lose?* I wondered. The elk's hesitation looked like fear to me.

That scene reminded me of some advice I've given myself on occasion: *Do it scared, Joan.* Because of past hurtful experiences, sometimes I'm afraid to jump over the next hurdle in my life. Afraid of doing it wrong, being ridiculed or feeling out of control, I'm tempted to stop short, not willing to experience the discomfort in order to jump over the obstacle toward healing and growth. So as I read Psalm 56:2 (*"whenever* I am afraid"*),* I relax. It's as though King David is saying, "God knows you'll feel afraid at times, so go ahead and *do it scared,* trusting that He'll be with you."

Lord, I'm weary of hearing that I shouldn't
be afraid. Thanks for understanding.

Make It Personal: I challenge you to "do it scared" twice this week. Each time you leap, imagine God jumping with you.

An Extravagant Price

For I am not ashamed of this Good News about Christ.
It is God's powerful method of bringing all who believe it to heaven.

Romans 1:16, *TLB*

Recently while writing about grace, respite and finding the fun, I felt heart-sick. In the span of a few days, I had listened as a friend shared her childhood sexual abuse story and as another admitted enduring verbal attacks by her husband for years. In a restaurant, I had heard a man curse his girlfriend over the phone and a mother scream shaming advice to her daughter. A ministry friend had shared about her work with battered prostitutes. I had spoken with loved ones enmeshed in serious relationship problems and with clients battling cancer. A colleague's mother had fallen, never regaining consciousness. Then I had read the morning headlines: "Toddler Abducted," "Campus Shooting," "Hurricane: Thousands Lost" and "Bomb Kills Soldiers."

All this distressing reality closed in on me. You've probably felt it, too. When the bad news around us merges with our personal disappointment, we can feel overwhelmed. We may over-work, over-exercise, over-eat, over-help or even over-drink in an effort to soften the pain. Underneath it all, we long for relief, for someone to understand and *do something*.

God is that Someone. He cares that we're surrounded by bad news. To show us that He's on our side, God paid an extravagant price: His Son. When we choose to accept God's costly gift, we're given comfort in our present sadness and a forever hope in heaven.

Lord, You soothe my heavy heart. I can't
express how much that means to me.

Make It Personal: How does God's gift bring you comfort and hope?

Reproducing Growth

*For God . . . will make it grow so that you can give away
more and more fruit from your harvest.*

2 Corinthians 9:10, *TLB*

I love flowers, plants, greenery—and taking photos of these colorful gifts from God. (For examples, visit my website, www.joancwebb.com.) One morning while walking through a beautiful, lush flower garden, I met the gardener. She pointed out and named each blossom, seedling and shrub. I saw dainty lilies of the valley, majestic purple irises, sun-splashed petunias, and geraniums the color of red crayons. My childhood favorite, the peony bush, appeared ready to burst into bloom.

This gardener showed me a hosta plant with its crisp, green and white variegated leaves. "Years ago, a friend gave me one small hosta sapling," she said. "I put it in the ground right here. That original plant grew and multiplied. And just look—now hostas outline the entire yard. Every season as each plant grows thicker, I break off new shoots and transplant them. Don't you just love the tiny flowers that spike from the center?"

As I walked away, I prayed, "Lord, make me like the hosta plant. Its refreshing green and white foliage adds character and depth to a garden wherever it flourishes. I want to be consistent year after year, too. And may I mature and grow a sufficient inner root system to join You in producing other strong, healthy plants."

*Growth produces growth, Lord. Please help me
develop and produce with consistency, health and balance
so that I can graciously help others grow and produce.*

Make It Personal: Jot down a way your growth has helped produce growth in others.

Messy Progress

Try to avoid going too far in doing anything. Those who honor God will avoid doing too much of anything.

Ecclesiastes 7:18, *NCV*

"Everything, everything, everything!" said my friend Sandi. "My unspoken motto is I should do and make *everything* right for *everyone*. Sounds nice, but something's haywire. Instead of feeling pleased, I'm resentful and worn out."

Like Sandi, some of us experience persistent inner turmoil. We want it all just right, yet we're anxious that we'll end up with nothing. Author Anne Wilson Schaef writes, "Our biggest fear is not knowing enough or not being enough. . . . We have become addicted to busyness, and if we are not busy we feel worthless, at a loss, and even frightened."[80] I identify.

I am making progress, though it's rather messy. As evidence, I submit the following diary excerpt: "I journaled, took a walk and rested on the hammock yesterday. It was not a wasted day! (I'm still trying to convince myself.) I called my husband to thank him for his support and he suggested we meet for lunch. I took a break and went. But my stomach felt knotted. Sometimes I'm still tempted to measure myself (and my day) by my activity level and the number of accomplishments I make. Slowly I'm learning, though, to enjoy others, life and God—and that's enough."

Lord, I want to honor You by doing less. Yikes, that almost sounds sacrilegious. I trust You for the continuing process, even when it feels so foreign to me.

Make It Personal: Plan a little hammock-type rest time for yourself this week. Mark it on your calendar. Then write yourself a "Congratulations!" note.

Do It Again

*"Master," Simon replied, "we worked hard all last night
and didn't catch a thing. But if you say so, we'll try again."
And this time their nets were so full they began to tear!*

Luke 5:5-6, *NLT*

From my window just now, I watched a golfer prepare and then strike his little white ball, only to flub it. It popped into the rough three feet to the right of where he stood. He slumped and shook his club. Then he walked over to the ball's new position and hit again. It sailed through the air, over the bunker and landed near the hole.

Sometimes we do "it" well. ("It" might be parenting, working, exercising, praying, teaching—or whatever.) Other times, even our best efforts yield less-than-stellar results and we slump inwardly.

I think Simon Peter probably wasn't thrilled when he and his coworkers worked all night with nothing to show for it. As a professional, surely he practiced the latest tricks of his trade. Still no fish. Yet when Jesus said, "Try again," Peter did.

We can, too. Like the disappointed golfer, we can walk a little farther, steady our stance and try again. Our actions won't always be flawless, since only God is perfect every moment of every day. Yet we can listen and obey His promptings to do it again.

*Lord, I'm bummed, but I'm willing to try again.
Please honor my efforts and bring worthwhile results.*

Make It Personal: *So you flubbed?* I challenge you to try again—consistently for the next three weeks. What will you do? Cement your decision by writing it here and calling a caring friend to share.

What's on Your Rock?

I planted, Apollos watered,
but God gave the increase.

1 Corinthians 3:6

Surrounded by candlelight, we shared stories of what God showed us during the retreat. The leader said, "Choose a rock from the pile on the center table." She explained that each rock had a word or phrase written on it, such as *Relationships, Work/Service* or *Emotions.* Then she added, "Reflect on your rock's topic, pray and when you're ready, leave your rock at the foot of this cross, signifying your intention to release this life area to God."

I chose a rock marked "Time and Money" and took it to the cross in surrender. Later, I journaled, "Lord, what did You wish to show me with the *Time and Money* rock?" The following inner dialogue resulted:

Lord: You don't need to let "time and money" dominate your ministry anymore.
Joan: Okay, Lord. But when there isn't enough time or money to do what You're calling me to do, then what?
Lord: Good question, Joan. What do you think?
Joan: Not sure. (Pause) Only thing I can think of is: *Do what you can, Joan . . .* (Pause) *. . . and I'll do the rest.* Lord, did You say that? Please confirm it with Scripture.

Since then, I've repeatedly heard in various ways, *Joan, do what you can and I'll do the rest.* With fresh eyes, I read Jesus' challenge in Matthew 6:33 to seek His kingdom first. Then I read Paul's words in 1 Corinthians: "I planted, Apollos watered, but God gave the increase." You and I do our God-given task and God does the perfecting. What indescribable relief.

Lord, You amaze me.

Make It Personal: What's written on your rock?

Change *Is* Possible

Just as Christ was raised from the dead through the
glory of the Father, we too may live a new life.

Romans 6:4

Teaching another workshop in one hour, I sit with participants over dinner when my cell rings. Strange—my husband knows I'm speaking. I excuse myself and call back.

"Hi, Hon. Where's your car key?" My mind races. *Richard's in Arizona; I'm in Missouri. Why would he need my key?* "Remember? Herb is driving your car this week. You were supposed to leave your keys." I rummage through my purse and hear a jingle-jangle. *Yikes! Keys! Now what?*

Re-entering the restaurant, I chuckle. A few years before, I'd have cowered in shame. Richard and I would have landed firmly in black/white mode, squelching all options and tensing up, and then silently (or not!) blaming one another. But today, that didn't happen. We all flexed and early Monday morning I sent the keys overnight air.

We *can* change our everything-must-be-just-right-or-else approach to life. I'm a grateful example. The transformation didn't happen overnight. It's been an imperfect process something like this: (1) *Acknowledge my need.* Awareness starts the journey. (2) *Admit my misconceptions.* For example: "I should foresee all problems and never make a mistake" or "My husband must always be happy with me." (3) *Replace my falsehoods with healthy thought patterns.* Observing how Jesus interacted is the best way to witness healthy living. (4) *Surrender the entire process to God.* (5) *Commit to feeling uncomfortable until the new ways become familiar.*

God did the energizing work through His Son's death and resurrection. Now we have the privilege of cooperating with Him for growth.

Lord, thanks for the promise of new life.

Make It Personal: Celebrate how you've changed.

Daily Sobriety

Therefore, prepare your minds for action, keep sober in spirit,
fix your hope completely on the grace to be brought to you
at the revelation of Jesus Christ.

1 Peter 1:13, *NASB*

"What do you think it means to be sober in spirit?" asked our workshop leader. The question intrigued me, so I looked up the word "sober" in the dictionary. The definition included these words: "not flurried, not excited, but self-possessed."[81] Sounding like the description of a recovering action-addict, it reminded me of what I longed to be: calm, consistent, less driven and better equipped to accept responsibility for my own life choices. I wondered, *How can I stay sober on a regular basis?*

I've discovered that one way is to focus daily on God's grace instead of on my own ability (or inability!) to make it all just right. Grace (joy-filled acceptance without expecting anything in return) is something like love.[82] I don't fully understand either one, and each time I have an *aha!* about love or grace, there's always another layer still to experience.

This morning, with a heavy heart for loved ones caught in self-defeating obsessions, I researched online and found this definition of "addiction": "the condition of being habitually or compulsively occupied with or involved in something."[83] So how do we stay sober?

Daily is how a new way of life becomes a habit. If we tried to tackle all our days at once, we'd become overwhelmed. Yet by taking one day at a time, we'll experience a lifetime of sober (responsible, balanced) living.

Lord, keep me sober just for today.
Tomorrow we'll start over again.

Make It Personal: What's your definition of "sober"?

Whose Expectations?

Am I now trying to win the approval of men, or of God?
Or am I trying to please men? If I were still trying to please men,
I would not be a servant of Christ.

Galatians 1:10

"Is your job difficult?" asked a journalist while interviewing a Chief of Staff to the President of the United States.

"No," replied the Chief of Staff. "I have only one constituent to please."

Just in the last week, I talked with several committed Christian women who struggle with trying to please the many people around them. Mother, father, sibling, spouse, child, friend, boss, pastor—it runs the gamut. Yet from personal experience and from my interactions with others, I've noticed that we walk an emotional-mental-spiritual tightrope when we attempt to juggle all the desires and demands of everybody around us. Usually we end up pleasing no one, while driving ourselves to overload. It gets exhausting. In fact, it's really a no-win way to live.

In the end, we who have chosen to follow Christ have only one constituent: God. And through our relationship with His Son, He offers us grace, mercy and unconditional acceptance, whether we're feeling spiritual or utterly human.

Lord God, I'm tired of trying to do and be what
everyone else wants. If I keep this up, I'll never become
the person You created me to be. I'm going to change my
pattern to do what I believe You designed for me.
Please give me wisdom-laced courage.

Make It Personal: Whose expectations are you trying to meet this week? List two action steps that will free you up.

Defusing the Fear

Blessed are you who are poor, for yours is the kingdom of God.
Blessed are you who hunger now, for you will be satisfied.
Blessed are you who weep now, for you will laugh.

Luke 6:20-21

When I decided that God wanted me to buck the status quo and change my over-trying and kowtowing, I felt scared. That's an understatement—I felt sick to my stomach every morning for almost two years straight. To help defuse the fear, I would ask myself, *In this situation, what's the worst thing that could happen?*

Depending on the circumstances, I responded with answers similar to these: *I could make a mistake. I might not succeed. My husband may withdraw. I might not make enough money. I could do something wrong and look ill prepared. (Perish the thought!) Others might disapprove. Somebody might even yell.*

Then I asked, *Would that be the end of the world?* To be honest, it sometimes felt like it would be. Yet I had come too far to give up merely because it seemed difficult, confusing or scary. Eventually my answer became, *I guess not. I know God accepts and loves me, no matter what.*

What made the underlying difference was this belief: *Although today I face unmet needs, pain and rejection, I have assurance of better things to come. Life isn't always fair or fun. I may cry sometimes now, yet one day I'll know complete satisfaction and joy.*

*Lord, You are my ultimate hope. I look forward
to being in heaven with You forever.*

Make It Personal: What brings you pleasure today and reminds you of heaven?

Unique Needs

And my God will meet all your needs according to his
glorious riches in Christ Jesus.

Philippians 4:19

"I just finished your book," said a friend. "I want to be just like you."
Mentioning a prayer I shared in one chapter, she asked, "How can I interact with God like that?"

After asking her what she really wanted (intimacy with God), I said,
"Kathryn, you have what you long for. I've watched you escape workaholism to bond with God through spontaneous flexibility—and that
fits you beautifully. God has created me to connect spiritually in part
through the exploration of words and concepts. We don't have to interact with God in the same way. He cherishes our authenticity."

"That's freedom, isn't it?" she responded. God is big enough to
meet each one of us according to our unique personalities and needs.

Some of us need to stop thinking and do,
　　while others need to stop doing and think.
Some need to stop asking and give,
　　though others need to cease giving and ask.
Some of us need to stop crying and smile,
　　yet others need to stop smiling and cry.
Some need to stop confronting and give in,
　　while others need to quit compromising and confront.
Some of us need to stop waiting and run,
　　though others need to stop running and wait.[84]

What do you need today?

Lord, thanks for allowing me to be myself in our relationship.

Make It Personal: Name a time when you felt really connected to God.
What was happening?

I Love You

*Fear not, for I have redeemed you; I have summoned
you by name; you are mine. When you pass through the waters,
I will be with you . . . When you walk through the fire, you will
not be burned; the flames will not set you ablaze. For I am the Lord,
your God . . . your Savior . . . you are precious and
honored in my sight, and . . . I love you.*

Isaiah 43:1-4

Do you long for relief, but aren't sure where to find it? Are you confused or skeptical about your options? Are you annoyed, even angry? Are you tired, doubting that you're even likable anymore? Do you worry what others will do if you change?

I was, too. I longed to be renewed, to feel, to think straight again, and to be released from the emptiness. I didn't know how. Then, with little remaining strength, I said, "I can't, Lord. Help me." And He did.

Yet change doesn't happen overnight. It isn't always easy. It takes time. As I've talked with other women, this seems to be the difficult part: trusting that healing and growth is a process and that it's okay. We all want transformation *now*! But hanging in there with God is worth it.

I'm grateful that after walking through the fire, I wasn't irreparably burned. I've been redeemed, given my life back, set free. I'm loved by God, the Savior. And so are you.

Lord, I don't know what's next.
Please help me.

Make It Personal: Write today's verse on an index card or Post-It Note and display it where you'll see it often.

Endnotes

1. *The Pocket Webster School and Office Dictionary* (New York: Pocket Books, 1990), c.f. "perfection."
2. Ibid., c.f. "perfectionism."
3. See Myron Rush, *Burnout* (Colorado Springs, CO: Victor Books, 1987), p. 13.
4. Robert J. Kriegel and Louis Patler, *If It Ain't Broke . . . Break It!* (New York: Warner Books, 1991), p. 53.
5. Joan C. Webb, *The Relief of Imperfection* (Ventura, CA: Regal, 2007), p. 156.
6. Myron Rush, *Burnout* (Colorado Springs, CO: Victor Books, 1987), p. 13.
7. Isaiah 40:28-31: "He will not grow tired or weary, and his understanding no one can fathom. He gives strength to the weary and increases the power of the weak. Even youths grow tired and weary, and young men stumble and fall; but those who hope in the LORD will renew their strength. They will soar on wings like eagles; they will run and not grow weary, they will walk and not be faint."
8. See the definition of "burnout" in yesterday's reading.
9. Jane Chestnutt, "All in a Woman's Day," *Woman's Day*, April 1, 2003, p. 6.
10. Melody Beattie, *The Language of Letting Go* (New York: Harper/Hazelden, 1990), p. 313.
11. Carol Travilla and Joan C. Webb, *The Intentional Woman* (Colorado Springs, CO: NavPress Publishing Group, 2002), p. 32.
12. Not his real name.
13. Jude 1:2: "Mercy unto you, and peace, and love, be multiplied" (*KJV*).
14. Carol Travilla, *Caring Without Wearing* (Colorado Springs, CO: NavPress Publishing Group, 1990), pp. 50-51.
15. Lawrence J. Crabb, *Inside Out* (Colorado Springs, CO: NavPress Publishing Group, 1988), p. 14.
16. Chapter title from Joan C. Webb, *The Relief of Imperfection* (Ventura, CA: Regal Books, 2007), p. 78.
17. Ibid., p. 155.
18. Lawrence J. Crabb, *Inside Out* (Colorado Springs, CO: NavPress Publishing Group, 1988), p. 199.
19. William Backus, *Telling Each Other the Truth* (Grand Rapids, MI: Bethany House, 1985), p. 169.
20. Melody Beattie, *Beyond Codependency: And Getting Better All the Time* (San Francisco, CA: Hazelden, 1989), p. 166.
21. "G225, *Aletheia*, Truth, Spiros Zodhiates, TH.D, *The Hebrew-Greek Key Study Bible, KJV, Lexicon to the New Testament* (Chattanooga, TN: AMG Publishers, 1984)), p. 1661.
22. CPAP stands for "Continuous Positive Airway Pressure."
23. David Stoop, *Living with a Perfectionist* (Nashville, TN: Thomas Nelson, Inc., 1987), pp. 167-168.
24. This and more information about eating disorders and treatment can be found at Remuda Ranch, www.remudaranch.com.
25. Statistics from the National Eating Disorders Association. http://www.edap.org/p.asp?Web Page_ID+320&Profile_ID=41138 (accessed December 2008).
26. *Webster's New World Dictionary of the American Language*, College Edition (New York: The World Publishing Company, 1966), p. 604.
27. Pat Springle, *Codependency* (Nashville, TN: W Publishing Group, 1990), pp. 49-58.
28. Healing Hearts Ministries International, www.healinghearts.org.
29. M. Scott Peck, *The Road Less Traveled: A New Psychology of Love, Traditional Values and Spiritual Growth* (New York: Simon & Schuster, 1978), p. 15.
30. Eugene H. Peterson, *The Message Remix* (Colorado Springs, CO: NavPress, Publishing Group, 2006), p. 1478.
31. I read William Backus' book *Telling Yourself the Truth* (Minneapolis, MN: Bethany House Publishers, 1980).

32. Not her real name.

33. Not her real name.

34. Brent W. Bost, MD, quoted in Keri Wyatt Kent, *Breathe* (Grand Rapids, MI: Revell Books, 2005), p. 23.

35. Brent W. Bost, MD, *The Hurried Woman Syndrome* (New York: Vantage Press, 2001).

36. "Boundaries help us define what is not on our property and what we are not responsible for. . . . Boundaries help us keep things that will nurture us inside our fences and keep things that will harm us outside." Dr. Henry Cloud and Dr. John Townsend, *Boundaries* (Grand Rapids, MI: Zondervan, 1992), pp. 14-15,18.

37. Myron Rush, *Burnout* (Colorado Springs, CO: Victor Books, 1987), p. 85.

38. My situation involved a business, but burnout can also happen in a ministry or family situation.

39. Robert Kriegel, *If It Ain't Broke . . . Break It!* (New York: Warner Books, 1991), p. 61.

40. Dr. Henry Cloud and Dr. John Townsend, *Boundaries* (Grand Rapids, MI: Zondervan, 1992), p. 199.

41. J. Keith Miller, *Hope in the Fast Lane* (New York: Harper Collins, 1999), pp. 142-143.

42. Mark Buchanan, *The Rest of God: Restoring Your Soul by Restoring Sabbath* (Nashville, TN: Thomas Nelson Publishers, 2007), p. 90.

43. Ibid., pp. 62-63.

44. Joanna Weaver, *Having a Mary Heart in a Martha World* (Colorado Springs, CO: Waterbrook Press, 2000), p. 9.

45. David Johnson and Jeff VanVonderen, *The Subtle Power of Spiritual Abuse: Recognizing and Escaping the Spiritual Manipulation and False Spiritual Authority Within the Church* (Grand Rapids, MI: Bethany House Publishers, 2005), p. 133.

46. TIAs are caused by the temporary disturbance of blood supply to a restricted area of the brain, resulting in brief neurologic dysfunction that persists for less than 24 hours. "Transient ischemic attack," Wikipedia.org. http://en.wikipedia.org/wiki/Transient_ischemic_attack (accessed November 2008).

47. Gary W. Chapman, "All I Ever Have to Be," Paragon Music Corp. c/o New Spring Publishing, Inc., Franklin, TN.

48. Miriam Elliott, PhD, and Susan Meltsner, *The Perfectionist Predicament: How to Stop Driving Yourself and Others Crazy* (New York: William Morrow and Co., 1991), p. 149.

49. Oswald Chambers, *My Utmost for His Highest* (New York: Dodd, Mead & Co., 1935), p. 9.

50. David Keirsey and Marilyn Bates, *Please Understand Me* (Del Mar, CA: Prometheus Nemesis, 1978), p. 1.

51. The God-shelf was introduced in *The Relief of Imperfection* by Joan C. Webb (Ventura, CA: Regal Books, 2007), p. 240.

52. Jane Chesnutt, "All in a Woman's Day," *Woman's Day* magazine, April 1, 2003, p. 6.

53. *Women of Faith Study Bible, NIV* (Grand Rapids, MI: Zondervan, 2006), p. 996.

54. Carol Turkington, *The Perimenopause Book* (New York: McGraw-Hill, 1998), p. 115.

55. Kevin A. Miller, *Surviving Information Overload* (Grand Rapids, MI: Zondervan, 2004), p. 15.

56. Dean Paton, "E-Serenity Now!" *The Christian Science Monitor*, May 10, 2004. http://www.csmonitor.com/2004/0510/p11s02-stct.html (accessed November 2008).

57. Ibid.

58. David Johnson and Jeff VanVonderen, *The Subtle Power of Spiritual Abuse: Recognizing and Escaping Spiritual Manipulation and False Spiritual Authority Within the Church* (Grand Rapids, MI: Bethany House Publishers, 2005), p. 197.

59. Joan C. Webb, *The Relief of Imperfection* (Ventura, CA: Regal, 2007), pp. 184-204.

60. You can read my story in *The Relief of Imperfection* (Ventura, CA: Regal, 2007), pp. 197-199.

61. Marsha Crockett, *Breath Through: Unearthing God's Image to Find the Real You* (Colorado Springs, CO: NavPress Publishing Group, 2008), p. 54.

62. Vonda Skelton, *Seeing Through the Lies: Unmasking the Lies Women Believe* (Ventura, CA: Regal Books, 2008), p. 46.

63 Oswald Chambers, *My Utmost for His Highest* (New York: Dodd, Mead & Co., 1935), p. 292.

64. Graham Melville-Mason, "Petr Eben," *The Independent,* October 27, 2007. http://www.independent.co.uk/news/obituaries/petr-eben-398044.html.

65. "Love is patient, love is kind. It does not envy, it does not boast, it is not proud. It is not rude, it is not self-seeking, it is not easily angered, it keeps no record of wrongs. Love does not delight in evil but rejoices with the truth. It always protects, always trusts, always hopes, always perseveres. Love never fails" (1 Corinthians 13:4-8).

66. Melody Beattie, *The Language of Letting Go* (San Francisco, CA: Hazelden, 1990), p. 249.

67. Although the verse refers directly to the Jewish people, I believe it represents His love for us, His adopted children, as well.

68. William P. Young, *The Shack* (Newbury Park, CA: Windblown Media, 2008), p. 196.

69. Steven R. Tracy, *Mending the Soul: Understanding and Healing Abuse* (Grand Rapids, MI: Zondervan, 2005), p. 24.

70. Vonda Skelton, *Seeing Through the Lies: Unmasking the Lies Women Believe* (Ventura, CA: Regal Books, 2008), p. 169.

71. William Barclay, *The Letter to the Romans* (Louisville, KY: Westminster John Knox Press, 3rd ed., 2002), p. 194

72. Myron Rush, *Burnout* (Colorado Springs, CO: Victor Books, 1987), p. 13.

73. Oswald Chambers, *My Utmost for His Highest* (New York: Dodd, Mead & Co., 1935), p. 125.

74. The Old Testament books Hosea, Joel, Amos, Obadiah, Jonah, Micah, Nahum, Habakkuk, Zephaniah, Haggai, Zechariah and Malachi.

75. For ideas to get you thinking of creative ways to spend time with God, read chapter 15 of my book *The Relief of Imperfection* (Ventura, CA: Regal Books, 2007), pp. 214-227.

76. Bobbie Liebermann, "Deep Breathing: It's Easy When You Don't Try," Discover Health online. http://health.discovery.com/centers/althealth/deepbreath/deepbreathe.html (accessed November 2008).

77. Jane Chesnutt, "All in a Woman's Day," *Woman's Day* magazine, April 1, 2003, p. 6.

78. Certified Life Coach Kristina Bailey, www.kirstinabailey.com.

79. "'Overwork' Killed Engineer," *The Arizona Republic*, July 10, 2008, Business section.

80. Anne Wilson Shaef, *Meditations for Women Who Do Too Much* (San Francisco: Harper & Row Publishers, 2004), p. 11.

81. *The Pocket Webster School and Office Dictionary* (New York: Pocket Books, 1990), p. 682, s.v. "sober."

82. Spiros Zodhiates, *The Hebrew-Greek Key Study Bible, KJV* (Chattanooga, TN: AMG Publishers, 1996), p. 1656. "Agape: a word not found in Classical Greek, but only in revealed religion. . . . Its benevolence, however, is not shown by doing what the person loved desires but what the one who loves deems as needed by the one loved. . . . God's love for man is God doing what He thinks best for man and not what he desires. . . . For man to show love to God, he must first appropriate God's agape, for only God has such an unselfish love."

83. *The American Heritage Dictionary of the English Language*, Fourth Edition (New York: Houghton Mifflin Company, 2003), s.v. "addiction." http://www.thefreedictionary.com/addiction (accessed November 2008).

84. Joan C. Webb, *The Relief of Imperfection* (Ventura, CA: Regal Books, 2007), p. 229.

Interacting with the Author

Joan C. Webb, a recovering workaholic, perfectionist and burn-out victim, communicates a message of freedom and renewal. In an age of over-choice and over-commitment, she shares refreshing news that God will "guide you always . . . satisfy your needs in a sun-scorched land" and make you like a "well-watered garden, like a spring whose waters never fail" (Isa. 58:11).

Joan is a freelance speaker, trainer and author who has authored or coauthored nine books, including *The Relief of Imperfection, The Intentional Woman* (coauthored with Carol Travilla), *Meditations for Christians Who Try to Be Perfect* and a four-book series titled *Devotions for Little Boys and Girls*. She also wrote study notes for several Old Testament books in Zondervan's *Women of Faith Study Bible*.

As a personal life coach and Intentional Woman Life Plan (IWLP) facilitator, Joan has accumulated hundreds of hours coaching and helping set people free from what holds them back to become who God gifted them to be. Joan's practical and interactive presentations include stories from her background in business, ministry and travel to the Middle East doing relief and development work. Joan and her husband, Richard, live in Chandler, Arizona, and have a daughter, a son and seven young grandchildren.

Contacting Joan

- For *Relief of Imperfection* updates, news, facilitator tips and a schedule of Relief of Imperfection retreats, workshops and presentations, visit www.reliefofim perfection.com.

- Concerning *The Intentional Woman* five-step process, visit www.intentionalwoman.com to view information, updates, facilitator tips and a list of speakers and facilitators in the growing Network of Intentional Woman Presenters.

- For information about Joan's life-coaching and life-planning or about her Intentional Writing seminars and workshops for beginning to intermediate writers, or to inquire about Joan's speaking, facilitating or training at your event, visit www.joancwebb.com or email her at joan@joancwebb.com.